Long Netting
& Net-Making

A Rabbit Catcher's
Guide

The author and Byron, a netting partnership.

Long Netting & Net-Making

A Rabbit Catcher's Guide

Jon Hutcheon

The Crowood Press

First published in 2006 by
The Crowood Press Ltd
Ramsbury, Marlborough
Wiltshire SN8 2HR

www.crowood.com

British Library Cataloguing-in-Publication Data
A catalogue record for this book is available from the British
Library.

ISBN   1 86126 821 1
EAN   978 1 86126 821 1

Dedication
To my long-suffering wife and children who allow me to pursue my
interests.

Acknowledgements
With thanks to all of those who are good enough to allow me on to
their property to pursue my interest; to my true friends in the
field, Graham and Nigel; and to the men who gave me such a good
start in country pursuits, Allen and Mark Ansell, whose friendship
and advice have never been forgotten.
    Finally, thanks to Bridport Nets who have supplied me with
twines and netting for several years, and have always provided a
friendly and excellent service.

Line artwork by Keith Field.

Typeset by Carreg Limited, Ross-on-Wye, Herefordshire

Printed and bound in Great Britain by
The Cromwell Press, Trowbridge

CONTENTS

INTRODUCTION

I am lucky enough to have been involved with nearly all types of field sports from an early age, and have grown up with a good understanding of all things relating to the countryside, and of how field sports and those who partake in them help to shape, nurture and preserve our glorious country landscape. It is also true to say that I enjoy shooting as much as the next man, especially rough shooting. Thus I have had glorious summer forays taking the humble yet wonderfully challenging wood pigeon from the rustic comfort of a makeshift hide; and in the course of my game-keeping experience I have stood shivering in the beating line, and have shot driven pheasant and partridge on many an occasion. All the above I have enjoyed, and I can still clearly recall particular days as though they were yesterday.

My real passion, however, is not in using a gun to bag my quarry, but rather nets, ferrets and dogs. Most of my sport is based around the prolific rabbit that I am happy to catch, given that it is a listed pest species and that its numbers at the time of writing are spiralling to levels that have not been seen since pre-myxomatosis days.

I have written this book with the aim of passing on to the next generation the skills of long netting, and the art of making your own nets. I strongly believe that both of these practices are on the decline and hope that I can help to promote them before they are lost in time forever. In addition I have included some information later in the book on trapping and snaring so that the netsman or woman can try and add a few extra rabbits to their bag when the netting is poor. I have not written this as 'an expert', but simply as someone who wishes to pass on to others what I have learnt, so they may enjoy field sports as much as I have done.

Rabbiting: The Beginning

When I turned eleven I was lucky enough to be given the opportunity to assist a local gamekeeper by beating on the 1,000 acre estate on which he worked. I had always taken part to some extent in country sports, as a great deal of my youth had been spent on a family friend's estate in the West Country. Like many, however, I did not really know how to increase my involvement in field sports locally, though managed to get a space on the beating line through a family friend who was already beating on a local estate. After a season of slogging up and down the South Downs with my trusty stick, I announced to my parents that this was the life for me, and that I wanted to become more involved with the country

The author out rough shooting, another of his passions.

life I was starting to love with an unrequited passion.

I was a very shy child, and did not have the courage to ask if I could help out on the shoot out of season, until I was pushed into doing so by my parents. The keeper was sympathetic to my cause, and I was asked to phone him. This I did, and soon my true sporting passion was to be developed. The keeper is someone I still regard with great respect today; he was, and still is, a passionate ferreter, and I was quickly smitten with the pastime of ferreting.

We used to go ferreting in a group of sometimes ten to thirteen people and would use over forty ferrets in a day, and catches of at least a hundred rabbits were common. Sometimes we would shoot them as they bolted, but mainly we would purse net the rabbits we were going out to catch as they were then less damaged and so easier to sell to butchers and game dealers.

The gamekeeper taught me how to despatch rabbits humanely, and also how to locate and retrieve a ferret down a hole by using a 'liner', a big old hob ferret attached to a line of cord on a collar. I also learned to use the more modern ferret-finder set, and how to set purse nets effectively so as to ensure the rabbits would be quickly rolled up in a ball. More importantly, however, the old gamekeeper taught me everything I now know about the countryside, and for that I will always be grateful to him.

I soon had my own ferrets, and so began to take an active interest in their welfare as well as the skill of working them. And I would like to say here that all those responsible for their care should remember that a ferret is not a tool, but a living creature, and must be fed, watered, cleaned out and handled regularly. If you treat your ferrets well, they will serve you well, and many a good rabbiting trip will be had by all; but if you neglect them and treat them with contempt, then that is how they will respond to you, and your ferreting will be short-lived because you will catch very few rabbits. Therefore it does not take a genius to work out that in the long run it pays dividends to treat your ferrets well.

Ferrets relaxing in their hutch during the summer months.

As my interest in ferreting grew, so did my interest in net-making, and at the age of thirteen I purchased a net-making kit at a game fair with the intention of making the world's greatest purse nets. Needless to say this did not happen overnight, and I think the first forty nets I made were probably the worst nets ever. My biggest problem was that I did not know anyone who made nets, so had to teach myself from the instructions that came with the kit. Eventually, and after much practice, I mastered the basics – and then discovered that my mentor made his own nets: at last there was someone who would show me what to do. I soon started producing good quality nets, but can honestly say that it has taken me all these years to make what I consider to be the ultimate purse net for use in the field.

You may ask why anyone would want to make their own nets when they could buy them relatively cheaply. Personally I find it more satisfying to use a hand-crafted product than a bought one, and if I am honest, I find hand-made nets to be of better quality than machine-made ones: to my mind, any hand-crafted product is bound to be of better quality than something that has been mass-produced.

I ferreted with Allen (the aforementioned gamekeeper) for the best part of nine years, and in that time moved up the ranks from ferret boy to top-rate ferreter (well, at least I hope I did!). During this time I worked for a spell as a gamekeeper and woodsman, but for various reasons gave it up as a full-time profession, carrying on with these pursuits rather as a semi-professional pastime.

I enjoyed going out in the countryside with Allen, but found it hard to keep up with all the ferreting and other activities, such as beating, when I had only a couple of days off a week. Finally I came to the conclusion that I would have to spend less time on the estate, and so I decided to 'go it alone'. After much letter writing I gained permission to conduct the rabbit control on a 90-acre (36ha) stud some thirty miles (50km) from home, and in just a short period of time built up a reputation of doing good quality work, and for being trustworthy and reliable. I soon had over a thousand acres (400ha) of ground to carry out rabbit and vermin control, as and when I pleased. I was shooting regularly and ferreting in the winter, and this suited me very well because my job was now quite flexible and allowed me plenty of time to get out and 'do my thing'.

This was when my other sporting passion became apparent. I had worked a little with lurchers in the company of my West Country friend, and many years previously had also tried my hand – rather badly – at long netting, both of which interests were now about to make a big comeback in my life. I dug out a long net that had been sitting in my shed for several years, mainly because when I had used it I had either got it tangled beyond belief or had set it so tight that any rabbits simply bounced off it. This net was only 25 yards (23m) long, but was to prove the making of my long-netting experience.

Like many others, I had seen a display at a country show, and this had given me a rough idea of the many ways I was going wrong; and so I set about practising setting and picking the net up until I felt confident enough to try it when ferreting. This I did, and duly bagged my first brace of long-netted rabbits on a cold December morning.

A hand-made hemp purse net.

My biggest problem was that I didn't know anyone who long netted locally, so had no tutor to show me how to go about it. Long netting, it seemed to me, was just about obsolete locally, and I was desperate for some advice and help. I had only a small booklet on the subject as a guide, so when I set about trying to catch rabbits at night, I did so in a really terrible fashion. But I never gave up, and I kept trying until eventually things started to shape up. It took me over a year finally to get the hang of things and to catch reasonable bags of rabbits during the hours of darkness – and indeed during the daylight hours, and at dawn. That was ten years ago, and now I long net regularly sometimes with a few shop-bought nets but mainly using my own hand-made nets – that seem to get better every year

CHAPTER 1

THE QUARRY, AND WHERE TO FIND IT

There are two things that any would-be rabbit catcher needs before he can start to catch rabbits: permission to hunt his/her intended quarry; and an understanding of the quarry so that it may be taken effectively.

Getting Permission

Getting permission to hunt rabbits you might think would be easy, when currently there are so many of these creatures scattered across the countryside; but sadly this is not the case. Landowners are, quite rightly, careful as to whom they allow access to roam on their property, and the beginner often finds himself in a 'catch twenty-two' situation, because generally those landowners want to see references from places to which you have already been allowed access. All is not lost, however, and contacts can be made.

I would firstly recommend joining a reputable field sports-associated club or society such as the BASC (British Association for Shooting and Conservation), or the Countryside Alliance or similar. Both of these organizations are known by most people, and offer insurance as part of their membership packages. This insurance is generally third party, and does not cover professional pest control for profit – so if you are doing anything for profit, check you have the correct cover first.

As a member of one of the above organizations you may find there are local members who may be willing to 'show you the ropes' and get you started. You could also try smaller local clubs, such as ferret or lurcher clubs: again, once you are a member, others may pass your details on to someone who may be happy to take you out. Joining a club that offers insurance is a good starting point, and does often help demonstrate to landowners that your intentions are serious.

My own way forward was to sit down with a copy of the local map and pick out farms where I had seen large numbers of rabbits, either on the farm itself or running around in its environs. I would then write to the farmer explaining my intentions, and post off the letter with a stamped addressed envelope. I guarantee that you will get more refusals than permissions, but do not give up, because eventually you may get lucky. You could also try nursery sites, as often they have more ground than you would expect and can provide very good sport. Other possibilities might be golf clubs or smallholdings – it would be a mistake to limit

The author and his lurcher with a morning's bag of ferreted rabbits caught on a smallholding.

yourself to just large farms as possible hunting spots.

Meeting the Landowner

Should you be lucky enough to be granted a meeting with a landowner with a possibility of gaining access to some ground, you should dress smartly, explain exactly what you are looking for, and establish what the landowner wants done in respect of any vermin control. If you only wish to ferret, make this clear, and don't make rash promises because if you do,

but then fail to deliver the goods, you will soon lose the ground. It is also imperative that if you are going to net, or to indulge in any other activities such as running dogs or shooting at night, you discuss this with the landowner and that he/she knows exactly what you intend to do.

I always make sure that I get any permission in writing from the landowner, and I keep in regular contact with him once permission is granted so he knows were I have been and what I have caught. Small gestures such as arranging where to park, and offering help at busy times of the year, are also often appreciated. Remember that farmers are busy people, and the last thing they want to be worrying about is what you are up to! Finally, once permission has been granted, only catch what you have been asked to, and do not do anything against the landowner's wishes as it might land you with problems and you could well lose your permission.

If you are netting and ferreting but you also have permission to shoot, be sure to pick up any empty shells and rubbish. If you are allowed to take a dog, you must be absolutely certain that it is stock-trained. Also, if it is only yourself who has permission to hunt on the ground, but you intend to take others with you, ensure the landowner is happy with this.

I find that it is best to be the sole permission holder, because several people having access can cause a whole host of problems: for instance, the rabbits will often become so harassed that they will move away, or they will become lamp shy if they are being chased at night, and this will ruin any long-netting plans from the outset. Then there is nothing worse than going to ferret some burrows only to find that Joe Bloggs has already done so the day before. Moreover, Joe may not have been as respectful of the countryside as yourself, and may have left any holes he has dug wide open. And it would be just your luck that the farmer turns up when you are there and accuses *you* of being the monster who has left the gaping three-foot hole in the meadow that his tractor has fallen into – and tells you curtly that your services are no longer required. Whilst Joe, none the wiser, lives to ferret another day.

Sometimes I go ferreting with a select few friends, but normally I work alone. If anyone does come with me I explain clearly that they must not disclose the location of the ground to anyone else, nor must they make any return visit unless I have asked them to at the farmer's request.

I have stuck to the above rules all my life, and I now have access to more than enough farms and often get invited to neighbouring properties – so I must be doing something right.

To conclude, getting permission is fundamental to your sport. Remember that every piece of ground is owned by someone, and to ferret or net it without having permission is poaching. You may think that it is permissible because you don't have a gun, but I can assure you that you are still *breaking the law* and can therefore be prosecuted. Ferreters, dog men (people who work lurchers and terriers) and long netters (the few remaining) are already often viewed with suspicion, thanks to a small minority who do poach – and to get caught poaching once will do more harm than to do a good job ten times over. I myself am certainly not blameless, and over the years have sometimes strayed to the wrong side of the fence, and occasionally let my dog run a rabbit on a field where really I should not have been. I am not proud of this fact, but I would add that when I have 'borrowed' – as I like to phrase it – rabbits, it has always been from ground that I know is not hunted by others and is not managed by a gamekeeper. My poaching escapades mainly took place during my teens on council-owned ground, or over public spots where many others did the same. I am not saying that this makes it all right, but at the time it certainly made it more justifiable to myself. However, I have learnt by my mistakes, and now that I am older and wiser I would never poach, and would certainly advise others to keep to ground where they *do* have permission to hunt.

Understanding the Rabbit

Now that we have established how to organize where to hunt your intended quarry, the next step is to understand the humble rabbit that you intend to catch. Rabbits were brought to our shores by the Romans and were a source of food and clothing from their fur. They were once a prized animal in this country, and to get caught poaching one could mean the loss of a hand or, later in history, deportation! There was also a time when rabbits were farmed, the person in charge being known as a 'warrener'.

When driven game shooting became more apparent in the late nineteenth century, the large fenced-in rabbit warrens disappeared and the rabbit quickly established itself within the wild. For years it was treated as a sporting animal until it became apparent that it was causing havoc to farm crops; as a result, in 1880 the Ground Game Act was introduced, which made it legal for tenant farmers to control rabbits damaging their crops and land.

Rabbiting was at its peak from 1900 to the 1950s, and many countrymen worked as full-time rabbit catchers using gin traps (now illegal), long nets and ferrets. Rabbits fetched a good price, and poaching – especially at night with long nets – became popular; indeed, many poorly paid workers poached merely to add a few pennies to the family income and some meat to the diet. In fact, long netting did not just appear from nowhere in the

1950s: it was a method of rabbit control that had been used for many years, certainly since the nineteenth century and probably well before that.

The Effects of Myxomatosis

Then in 1953, disaster hit the rabbit world in the form of myxomatosis. The disease is carried by the rabbits' fleas, and as rabbits live mainly underground, it spread rapidly through the country and wiped out 98 per cent of the rabbit population. A few, mainly rogue bucks (males) and weaker followers, lived above ground and thus avoided the disease, and in time these rabbits bred, and by the late 1970s the population was on the increase. Now, in 2005, the rabbit population is as high as I have seen it in over sixteen years, thanks to ideal breeding conditions, and the rabbit is once again on the top of the pest species needing control. A disease known as viral haemorrhagic disease (VHD) did pose a threat to the rabbit population during the mid-1990s, but thankfully it has not as yet had the effect that many thought it would, of wiping out the UK's population. It did take hold in places, especially in the counties of the South West, but I have heard that even there, rabbits are coming back in healthy numbers.

Myxomatosis – commonly known as 'myxi' – is easily spotted, because the rabbit's face becomes bloated with pus-filled sores, especially around the eyes, whereas VHD has no external symptoms but affects the rabbit internally, killing it within forty-eight hours. However, rabbits with myxi often recover within two weeks of infection. Even so, I should add that, although many farmers despise rabbits, I know of none who enjoy seeing a rabbit suffer a long and painful death through disease, especially an affliction as evil as 'myxi'.

Habitat

Rabbits generally live underground in systems known as burrows or warrens. A burrow is a small version of a warren of perhaps up to twenty holes; anything larger than this would be a warren. In Sussex were I live there is a vast system of burrows and warrens: some on the chalky downs go down to depths of 15ft (5m) and more; burrows dug into inland clay are smaller, and go no deeper than a few feet. The most significant in size and complexity are situated on sandy soil found inland from the rolling downs, where they go down over 15ft (5m) and might consist of over two hundred holes. These I do not dare to ferret, and tend to trap and shoot instead. Some rabbits live above ground, especially in very thick wooded areas, but generally they are ground-dwelling creatures.

A Pest Species

Rabbits can do extensive damage to forestry and crops, which is why they need to be controlled. They will also burrow into fields, and this can pose a risk to horses grazing the area, as they could put

Rabbit damage on the chalky South Downs.

their foot down a hole. I have seen orchards of apple trees stripped of bark by rabbits, and fields of wheat eaten almost flat in places.

Because rabbits cause so much damage they do need to be controlled, and by law a landowner has an obligation to control the rabbit population on his property. Rabbits breed – well, like rabbits! In theory, in a two-year period one pair of rabbits and their offspring, providing they all survived, could be responsible for over three thousand rabbits – though in reality a wild rabbit would be very lucky to live longer than a year old.

The main problem today is that whereas in the past rabbits would only breed during the warmer months of the year, now they breed all year round, although to a lesser degree in the winter. They do fall victim to foxes and buzzards, stoats and weasels, and mink, and badgers will also sometimes take rabbits; but wild predators in fact account for a very small percentage of the rabbit population in the UK. Thus it is easy to see, and justify, why rabbits need to be controlled, because if left to their own devices they would soon over-populate.

The most important thing to remember if you do intend to catch rabbits, or indeed any living creature, is to respect your quarry and to despatch it humanely and quickly. The best ways to do this are explained briefly, later on in this book.

The hedge in the photo has been so undermined by rabbit damage that it is starting to collapse.

CHAPTER 2

THE LONG NET

If I have not yet managed to put you off starting to long net, and you are still keen to venture forth on a dark, cold winter's night with the intent of returning home with a bag full of coneys – then please read on.

Later on in this book I shall suggest when and where to net for optimum returns, but first let me explain the basics of a long net, and what you will need to get started. Let us assume for the time being that you do not intend to make your own nets, but are going to purchase them ready assembled: so what can you expect for your money?

Firstly, most shop-bought long nets

A 6oz (centre) and a 4oz (right) long net. Both are 50yd (46m) long and can be seen complete with debris, indicating they have been recently set.

come in a material that you will know, namely nylon, a man-made fibre – and in net form it is the very devil for attracting debris. Most shop-bought long nets come in two strengths: 4oz (113g) and 6oz (170g) nylon. The 4oz has a breaking strain of 40lb (18kg), and the 6oz a breaking strain of 60lb (27kg), so the latter is more than effective when set to capture rabbits. You can also get 10oz (284g) nylon nets that are excellent when you are working areas with a lot of cover that can snag the nets up – however, a 10oz net will weigh around four times as much as a 4oz net, so using them can be very tiring. In all honesty, using the 10oz long net is impractical, given its weight, and I only ever run these nets in really overgrown areas as a last resort.

A shop-bought net will generally come in three lengths: 25, 50 or 100yd (23, 46 or 91m). The 25yd net is a good net for the

The author with a handmade, 75yd net in 4oz nylon.

person who wants to use it only occasion-ally, for instance as a stop net when fer-reting, and it is a good size for a beginner to get used to the feel of a net; however, I would suggest that for netting at night, the best size would be from 50yd upwards, depending on the size of the fields you intend to net, and how much netting you intend to do. Personally I find that 100yd nets are difficult to handle and easy to lose control of, and so if I do have to buy a net, I would opt for one 50yd in length. Needless to say, given the amount of netting that I do, this is not always possible, and I do run nets of 100yd and even 200yd (183m) in length. When making nets, however, I go for 75yd (69m) in length, as I find these are easy to handle, carry and set out in the field when working alone, as I often do.

As already mentioned, the main disad-vantage of nylon is that it tangles so read-ily; but apart from this, I can honestly find no fault with it. It is rot-proof, so although it does need drying out, it will last for a very long time. It is also rela-tively light, so it is quite feasible to carry a reasonable amount of it without too much trouble.

Construction of a Long Net

Let us say, for argument's sake, that you have decided to buy a 50yd (46m), 6oz (170g) nylon net, and are all ready to go out and make your purchase. What should you get for your money, and where do you get it from? There are several com-panies across the country that sell long nets: some will sell a basic net, the others a slightly better net that they have worked on themselves.

To explain this is simple. Most nylon nets are machine made, and in many cases the supplier you go to will sell you a net that has come direct to him ready assembled. By this I mean it is ready to take from the shop and use, its draw cords and runners having been already attached in the factory it has come from. Some suppliers, however, purchase the mesh for the netting, and then fit the drawer cords to the netting themselves. These nets are often slightly better quali-ty and a little more expensive, but they are well worth the investment.

The meshes for a long net are attached to a top and a bottom cord, each called a runner, so for example a 50yd net will be set on a top runner of 50yd and a bottom runner of 50yd. The runners on your shop-bought net will generally be of a thicker type of white nylon: it is a cord similar to those used on window blinds, and is very strong and durable.

Needless to say, if the net mesh were no more than 50yd long when stretched its full length, it would effectively be so tight that rabbits would bounce off it; accordingly, all long nets contain what is known as 'bagging' or 'slack'. Bagging is basically extra netting that makes up the volume of the net so that it is not tight when set, and can thus enmesh the rab-bits that run into it.

I would suggest that the minimum amount of bag that a 50yd-long net should contain is no less than 25yd – and we are talking a real minimum here, one that would be only just enough to hold rabbits. Realistically, however, you want at least a yard of bag to every yard of net, so a 50yd-long net should have 50yd of bagging in it in order to work in any way near an effective manner. Ideally the more bag that you have in your nets, the more chance you will have of holding

A net that has been set: note how the netting blows inwards, indicating how the bag/slack netting sits between the net's runners.

rabbits, and I would go so far as to say that for the ultimate performance you want at least 2yd (1.8m) of bag to each yard of slack.

If you buy a factory-produced net it is likely to have about half a yard (0.45m) of bag to each yard (0.9m) of net, whereas a net that has had the runners added to it and comes from a reputable supplier will be more likely to hold a yard of bag to each yard of net – and it may even have 1.5 to 2yd (1.4 to 1.8m) of slack. If you are buying a net and are not sure how much slack it holds, just ask – and if you are not happy that the net holds enough slack,

then ask for some to be added in: most net suppliers are extremely helpful and will want to make sure you get the right product for your needs; after all, if you are satisfied, you will probably return for more nets in the future.

Net Colour

Most nets are produced in brown or green, and this is a perfectly acceptable colour for a net. Many rabbit catchers say that a net must be dark or rabbits will see it and not go towards it, but I do not agree with this; I have run long nets in white

A 6oz, 50yd net, set as a stop net around a covert for some daytime netting; note how the pegs are set at a slight angle to help take the strain of the quarry hitting the net.

A rabbit caught up in a net; it is clearly visible how the bag/slack has balled around the rabbit.

and blue, and these have taken just as many rabbits as my green and brown ones. A white net can easily be dyed a different colour, if you wish.

Net Height and Mesh Size

The final thing to mention is the overall height and size of your net. The width of most standard machine-made nets is between fifteen and seventeen meshes, each of 2in (5cm) diameter; however, because a 2in mesh will stretch to 4in (10cm) in diameter, this means that when the net is stretched out it will measure between 5 and 5.5ft (1.5 and 1.6m). A net of this size will give a maximum setting height of 3 to 3.5ft (0.9 to 1m), because when you set the net it will not be stretched out to its full height – if it were, it would have no bag whatsoever. These meshes will entangle a full-grown rabbit, but will allow young rabbits to pass through with ease, to grow larger for another day.

Not wishing to appear too fussy, I

A net stretched out on its runners to show the width of the net with the bag/slack spread.

The same section of netting pulled tight, with all of the slack/bag removed.

prefer a mesh size of $2^{1}/_{8}$in (5.3cm), because a rabbit's head will fit through it and it will become really entangled; it was always the preferred mesh size of the old-time rabbiter. I also have a few nets with $2^{1}/_{4}$in (5.6cm) mesh size; but anything larger than this would, I believe, prove too large, and rabbits would be able to pass right through the meshes.

I feel it is worth mentioning that in nylon nets, the meshes will actually stretch to a degree, and in most cases a standard 2in mesh will, over time, allow extra play and will often stretch to about $2^{1}/_{8}$in in size.

Making Your Own Nets

Should you decide to make your own nets, as I did, there are several options open to you. Net-making is covered later in this book, and indeed you could make your own long nets by hand – but this is a long and time-consuming task. By far the easiest method is to buy what is known as sheet netting, and to cut it to the size you require. Sheet netting normally comes in lengths of 150yd (137m), and in the standard 2in (5cm) mesh size. Once you have the netting, it is basically a case of attaching your runners to the net.

I like to use 75yd (69m) nets, so 150yd of sheet netting gives me enough netting to make one net with plenty of bag in it; and if I want a net with more bag than a yard per yard, it is simply a case of joining two lots of sheet together. The runners must be cut from one single length for the top and bottom runner, so for a 75yd net I would cut two lengths to 75yd each – if the runners are cut from shorter lengths and tied, they will snag and

make the net worthless. Attaching the runners is a simple but time-consuming task, and again, is covered later in this book.

The first time you make your own net is always the worst, but once you have done a couple, you start to wonder what seemed so difficult! I find that nylon nets are ideal for basic netting during the day or night, though they do seem to pick up every twig and leaf around; this is another reason why I prefer to run nets no larger than 75yd, as they are much easier to deal with than a 100yd net. Of course, on large runs I have to use longer nets or I would be constantly joining nets together, which would be impractical.

A section of a long net set around a rabbit burrow when ferreting; note the lack of bag/slack in the net: this will allow rabbits to bounce off the net and to escape with ease.

When using long nets for ferreting I often use a net measuring around 30yd (27m). These nets are easy to handle, and because I seldom need more than 100yd in total, it is an easy task to take three or four nets with me. My ferreting nets are different to those I use at night, because they hold at least $2^{1}/_{2}$yd (2.3m) of bag to every yard of slack. This is purely because when ferreting, I find that everything happens so fast that I like a net that really balls up a rabbit with ease.

The nets I use for night netting and my day sets are all set with at least a yard of bag per yard of net; this I find is generally more than adequate for my requirements. I do have some nets with 2yd (1.8m) of bag per yard of net, and use these mainly on ground where I know that the rabbits are going to be really prolific and the extra bag will be needed to ensure they get balled up tight enough.

As well as my nylon nets I also have some nets that are made from hemp and spun nylon. Hemp is a natural material, and its drawback is that when wet, it will rot; it also becomes very heavy. Spun nylon is a 'woollen' form of nylon, and although rot-proof, it, too, becomes very heavy if it is wet. I use these nets purely for areas of cover where it would be impossible to use standard nylon, which would tangle; hemp and spun nylon almost never tangle, and are extremely easy to handle. I must confess, however, that since discovering 10oz nylon I am starting to use this in preference to hemp and spun nylon, because it, too, is very easy to handle, and is, of course, rot proof. It is possible to buy hemp and spun-nylon long nets 'off the peg', but they are generally made to order and are hand made, and so the price can be two or three times that of a standard nylon net.

The final difference in my own nets as compared to a shop-bought net is that I use a much heavier bottom runner: I generally use a thicker nylon of about $^{1}/_{4}$in (6mm), which can be purchased from most hardware stores. I use these runners because I find the added weight at the bottom of the net helps to ease the setting of the net and its ability to hold rabbits. Another alternative is to use a leaded bottom line, basically a cord with a thin inner line of lead that weights the bottom of the net down.

Supporting the Net

The next question is how to support the net. The net is basically set to form a wall between the rabbits and the place they are making a run for, so some sort of peg or stake is needed to support the net at intervals to ensure that it stays upright. Opinions vary as to how high a net should be set. I know many who set it to a height of, say, 3ft (0.9m), so the runner is just resting on the ground. However, set like that I find that rabbits will often slip under the runner without even touching the net, so I prefer to set my nets at a height of 18 to 21in (45 to 52cm – depending on the ground I am working on), with at least 1ft to 1.5ft (0.3 to 0.5m) of netting being left on the ground, so that any rabbits have to actually run over the netting and therefore stand little chance of escape.

You will need to peg your net at intervals so that it stays upright; this is generally at points about 5yd (4.6m) apart. If you peg at distances any further apart than this, it often means that if a large number of rabbits hit the net they will pull the peg loose and knock the net down. This can, of course, vary depending on the ground you work, and on very soft ground where the peg goes in really deep you may get away with pegging every 8yd (7.3m) – although I must admit I find this distance a little *too* much for my liking; the furthest I would set my pegs apart, even on the softest of ground, is probably 6 to 7yd (5.5 to 6.4m).

Thus for a 50yd (46m) net, if you were to peg it every 5yd (4.6m) you would need about ten pegs. At this point the bag of the net comes back into play, because you will need to ensure that when set, the bag is evenly spread between the pegs; otherwise you will end up with an area that is set too tight and will not operate properly, because without any slack, any rabbits will bounce off it. Remember, it could happen that two or three rabbits hit one 5yd section of mesh, so you need enough bag in each section to enmesh that number; that is why you need at least a yard of bag to each yard of net. To my mind, bag or slack netting is the most essential

A net set on a hazel peg; the bottom runner is free running, and the top is pulled tight and hitched to support the net.

Setting a net on to the pegs.

aspect of successful long netting, and must never be overlooked.

Pegs

So what can you use for your pegs, and how big should they be? If you opt for my method of setting your net low, with a certain amount of it at ground level, I would recommend a peg of around 23in (58cm) long: this gives a good 3in (7.5cm) to push into the ground and enough length left to secure the net – at the very most I would use a peg of 26in (65cm) long, especially if the ground were very soft and a little

more support were needed. Short pegs are also a lot easier to carry than long ones. I am mystified by the netters who use pegs that measure 4 or 5ft (1.2 or 1.5m) in length, as it must be very hard to attach a net on to these pegs, or to carry them without them clanging about.

The traditional material to make pegs for long netting is hazel that has been cut and dried, and coated with a protecting agent such as linseed oil or a wood varnish. I point my hazel pegs on the bottom, and on the top cut a small 'v' shape about an inch down to support the top runner. I finally round the top so that it is nice and

Net set at 5yd intervals with the slack visible between each peg.

smooth to push on. Furthermore I have fitted rubber walking-stick ferules to the tops of some my pegs, so as to make pushing them into the ground a lot easier: the rubber is much more forgiving on the hands than cold hazel.

The two alternatives that can also be used with great effect are carbon-fibre poles, sold by most net manufacturers. These are not cheap, at about £3 each, but they are very strong and light to carry. It is not possible to cut a 'v' into them, but a simple solution is to attach some carpet tape about an inch from the top to stop the top runner from slipping. The second alternative is to use electric fencing poles. I use the pigtail type, and I simply cut the pigtail off and cut the 'v' into the top, as with hazel. These are slightly cheaper, at about £12 for ten.

There are still other alternatives, but remember that whatever you use must be strong enough to withstand a rabbit or rabbits hitting a net attached to it at speed. You also want something light and easy to carry, so steel rods, for example, would be just too heavy. Also bear in mind the thickness of your pole: my hazel pegs are no thicker than $^{1}/_{2}$in (13mm) in diameter, and given that some nights I may have to net 300yd (274m) and more in one go, I can end up carrying a lot of pegs!

The Anchor Pin

The final component that you will need to operate your net is an anchor pin. Some opt not to use one, but I find it a useful part of the net that makes picking it up and securing it a lot easier than some of the other methods. The anchor pin is generally made from steel, and is basically a length of pointed steel of between 6 and 10in (15 and 25cm), depending on preference. The pointed end is pushed into the ground, and the other end is shaped into a circle of between 2 and 6in (5 and 15cm) in diameter. This end is used to secure the runners, and must be completely sealed with a good weld. If this is not done the runners will slip off the pin, and also you will find that the meshes of the nets will get tangled over the pin.

One anchor pin is attached to each set of runners at each end of the net. As the name suggests, the pins act as anchors to hold the net in place and to keep it secure. They can also be used to pick the net up, and that is why the rings must be welded, as mentioned above. Some prefer to run their nets free and to avoid anchor pins altogether, and indeed there is one method of netting that does not require any pins (we will cover this later). But certainly I find that on a standard long net, anchor pins are a must and make the whole operation a lot smoother.

Gathering a net up onto an anchor pin.

CHAPTER 3

STARTING IN THE FIELD

Carrying your Net

It is to be hoped that you now have a basic understanding of the workings of the long net, and will be ready for the next step of actually running your net out in the hope of catching some rabbits.

For the purpose of netting we first need to establish the basics of setting the net, and also of how to carry your net to and from your selected site. Firstly we will deal with the transportation of your net and pegs. Most netting takes place after dark, and it is important to be as quiet as possible so as not to give your quarry any indication of what you are doing. Despite the conviction of many people, rabbits are not silly, and will pick up on every strange sound and movement. Therefore you need to carry your kit in such a manner that it will not flap and bang around.

I find there are two ways of doing this. The first is more suitable to a two-man netting team, and consists of the nets being carried in a bag that can be worn comfortably over the shoulder so the net can be removed and run out with ease. Ideally the bag should therefore have no more buckles or zips than is absolutely essential, and should be as basic as possible. I use small ex-army bags that cost

about £1 each; I cut the buckles, and attach a piece of old seat-belt as a strap to the rear of the bag, which then sits over my shoulder quite comfortably and hang to my front, allowing me to remove the net easily for running out.

The pegs are carried separately in a quiver that is basically made from an old jeans or cord trouser leg, and again has a length of seat-belt attached to it as a strap and thus can be worn over the shoulder. As already mentioned, this method is ideal for a two-man team, as one runs the net out whilst the other holds the quiver and sets the pegs.

For the solo netter I find the best method is the one that most serious netsmen seem to opt for – or certainly the ones that I have come across. This is the netter's coat, and it can easily be adapted from most basic coats to suit the netter. First of all any zips and buttons should be removed, to prevent unnecessary snagging of the net. I use a long wax coat with just one centre zip that is taped over to stop it snagging or clattering.

Next you need to sew one or two large pockets at about waist level into the inside of the coat; these will be used to carry the nets. I use old pillowcases for this, as they are light but strong; some people use old sacking, but remember to

The author with pegs in a home-made quiver and 200yd of netting held securely in a small carrying bag.

The author in his netting coat showing the internal pockets and the quiver attached to the inside of the coat.

use a durable rot-proof material that will not make a noise if it rubs against you.

Finally on the inside of the coat you will need to sew in a quiver to hold your pegs. As I am left-handed I have mine sewn into the right-hand side so that I can reach across to it. Again, this is sewn in at about waist level, but make sure that it will not clatter the pegs against your leg when you walk.

Needless to say, all the other clothing you wear should be snag proof, with any buttons or zips removed or taped over. Footwear should also be taken into account; I dislike Wellington boots so wear good strong walking boots that are extremely comfortable in the field, but again ensure that laces and eyelets will not snag on the net. If you require gloves and a hat, I would opt for the woollen skull cap because this will not flap around; and fingerless gloves are ideal, as you can still easily grasp the net and any other equipment.

Setting your Net

Before we can proceed to some netting situations, you need to know the basics of setting and picking up your net. I would suggest that before you use your net you run it out in an open area to its full length, and attach your anchor pins to each end.

Simply pass the bottom runner at each end through the loop on the anchor pin, then do the same with the top runner at each end. The next step is to tie the runners securely in place; the real experts

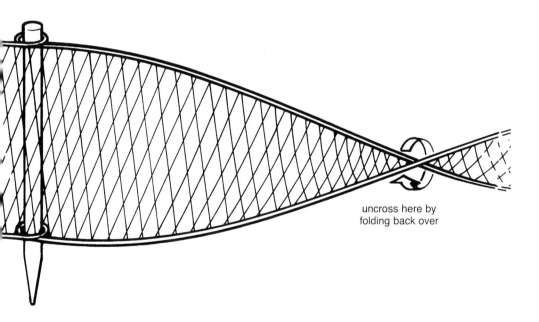

uncross here by
folding back over

If the net runners become twisted one over another you will need to ensure that they are unwrapped, otherwise the net will end up being set with large gaps between it.

would sew the bottom and top runner together where they joined through the anchor pin, as it was often felt that a knot would snag the net. I must confess that I do not do this, and knot my top and bottom runners together – and I have never had any problems with them snagging.

Once you have secured the runners, walk the length of your net and ensure that the top and bottom lines are not twisted; this is the most common problem with a long net, and one that you will probably encounter after you have picked up your nets when out for real in the field. By twisting I mean that the top line is folded over the bottom line and is crossed; this needs to be rectified, because otherwise your net will be set with gaps throughout it and will be useless. You must ensure that both lines are untwist-

ed, and then spread the slack along the net as evenly as you can.

After you have done this it is time to attach your pegs to the net, as already mentioned, at every 5yd (4.6m). This will give you the opportunity to see what your net looks like when it is set, and you will need to know this before trying it out for real. Attaching the pegs is an easy process: simply take your peg and push the bottom end between the bottom runner and the bottom of the net, being sure not to snag any of the netting. Then attach your top runner to the peg by doing a half hitch right and then a half hitch left. The top runner should become relatively tight, the bottom runner should be much looser.

You may find that you need to use more than the two half hitches on your early attempts, and that is fine; the main

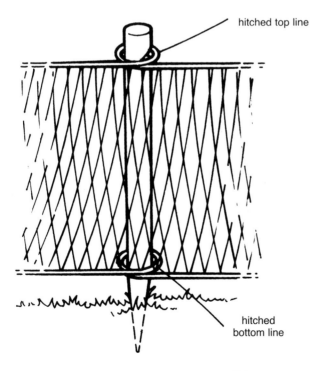

hitched top line

hitched bottom line

Attaching the net to the peg by hitching the top and bottom runners to the peg.

The author's preferred method of attaching the runners to the peg: the top runner is hitched, but the bottom runs freely between the peg and the netting.

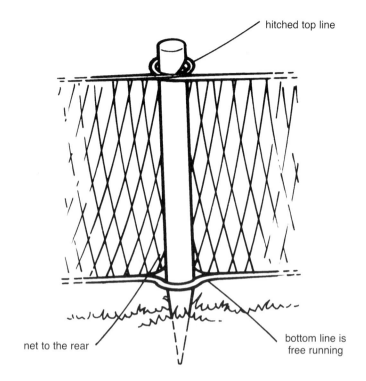

hitched top line

net to the rear

bottom line is free running

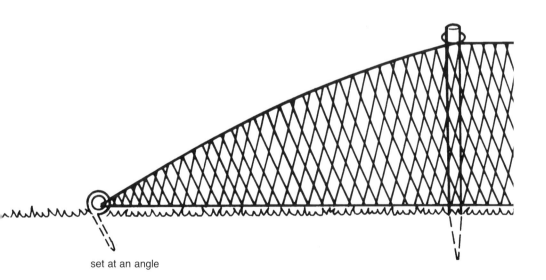

set at an angle

The first section of a set net, indicating the anchor pin's role of holding the net in place.

thing is that the top line is tight and the bottom line is relatively slack, and that the netting itself is evenly spread between the pegs. You do not want the netting to bunch up around the pegs, so as you set the net you can slide the netting evenly as you go; this is why it is important that the runners do not have any knots on them, as they will stop the net from spreading. Once you have attached the anchor pins and the pegs as described above, the net can be bagged up, and your next attempt at running it out will be with the anchor pins in place and in the field, hopefully to bag rabbits.

When going out on your first solo trip, the easiest method is to run the net out to its full length; then, as you did on your practice set, walk back and attach the pegs. Once you have managed to set the net, you can try attaching your pegs as you go, which is a much quicker method, and the one that ideally you want to use in the field. The disadvantage of running your net out and then walking back and pegging it, is that the net will pick up debris that without doubt will snag. The method of attaching your pegs as you go is the same as above, except that you will keep the net stored in your bag or pocket,

Setting the anchor pin to the ground; the first step to running out a net.

Running the net out and spreading the bag/slack.

Attaching a peg via two half-hitches to the top runner.

and only run out at any one time the section you wish to peg.

Your first peg and last peg should be about 5yd (4.5m) from the anchor pins, and you will notice that the netting tends to rise from the pin to the first peg in a 'V' shape. This should also be the case with the last peg and pin. The rest of the net should look somewhat like a wall of meshing, and if correctly set, the meshing will billow in the wind and you will clearly be able to see the bagging between each set peg.

To run a net out solo from a bag or netting pocket will mean that you have to slip it from the anchor pins beforehand. An alternative, and by far the easiest, method after practice – and believe me, it takes a lot of practice! – is to hold the supporting anchor pin and netting in one hand and to attach the peg with the other. If the ground is hard, simply push the supporting pin into the ground to hold the spread netting, and use both hands to secure the peg.

One final point I must make about net setting concerns the terrain you are netting on. It is common sense that if you are going to be netting ground that is perhaps covered in fresh stubble or is thick with thistles, it will be pointless to run the net out first and then peg it, because it will just become a mass of tangles. In this situation you will either have to pre-set your net, a method that we will look at later, or you will have to run it and peg it as you go, as I often do.

The last alternative is to work with somebody else, as a team – but even if you do this you will probably still end up with snags, as there is always a short distance between the man running out and the person pegging, so even this is not foolproof. This situation will also apply i[f] you are netting in woodland during the day, or around thick cover – so be pre[-]pared!

Picking Up Your Net

To pick your net up, the easiest metho[d] for the beginner is to unhook the top lin[e] along the whole length of the net, the[n] remove one of the anchor pins. Holdin[g] the pin in one hand, reach an arm'[s] length along the net and take hold of th[e] netting and top and bottom runner, the[n] place this over the point of the ancho[r] pin. Hold this in place with your thum[b] and finger, leaving the rest of your han[d] to hold the pin in. Repeat this process fo[r] the length of the net until you come t[o] about 3yd (2.7m) from the end anchor pin[.] Remove this pin from the ground, and us[e] the 3yd of netting to wrap around th[e] main body of the net that has been col[-] lected up and secured to the anchor pin.

Your net should now be in a tight bun[-] dle, with one anchor pin passing throug[h] the centre of it, and the second on th[e] outer side. The net can then be place[d] back into its bag or pocket. You will nee[d] to ensure that the anchor pins are place[d] inside the bag/pocket so that the ring is a[t] the bottom, because if you put it in poin[t] downwards, the net can slide off th[e] anchor and become tangled. A good wa[y] to avoid this is to carry a strong elasti[c] band or piece of cut inner tube that can b[e] wrapped around the two anchor pins t[o] hold the net securely and to prevent i[t] sliding.

You will no doubt find that when yo[u] pick up your net, even on the most open o[f] spaces, some debris will become snagge[d]

Lopping the net on to the anchor pin.

Pulling the net on to the pin, ensuring the slack is still held in place.

Folding the net on to the anchor pin; note that the pin is held upwards to stop the netting falling from the pin.

within the net. You need to try and remove this as you go, because if you leave it in, it will soon tangle the net. Leaves and grass will often shake out, but twigs will cause real problems. The best way to overcome this is to leave the net attached to the pegs when you pick it up, so that it is always raised from the ground. The only difference to picking the net up in this manner is that you will need to unhook the top runner as you go, and the novice may find that he doesn't have enough fingers and thumbs to hold everything at once. However, this is something that you will master in time, with practice.

If you are not running out your net alone, then setting and picking up is a much quicker process, as one person can run the net out and the other can spread the slack and attach the pegs as you go. The same applies to picking up the net. Here, the important part is to ensure that the net is picked up without the top and bottom runners crossing over, as this makes the net very hard to reset when you next intend to use it. The best option for the novice is to start off with a short 25yd (23m) net, and to master this before attempting to run out a 50yd (46m) net or larger in the field.

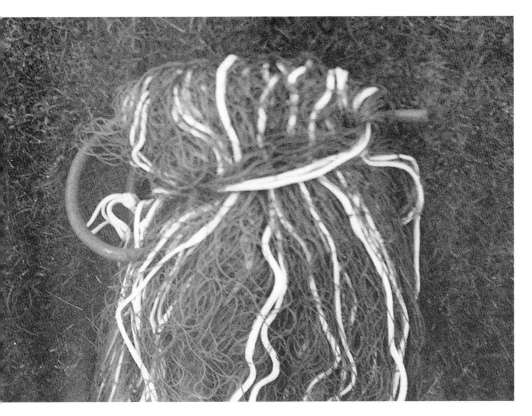

The net bagged up to the anchor pin and secured via wrapping the last 2 to 3yd of netting around the gathered netting.

Once you have practised running out a small net in the open and in daylight, and feel quite confident with it, it is to be hoped that soon you will try using it in the field to catch live quarry. I personally prefer to net alone, since as of yet I have not found anyone who can assist in setting a net at night without making a lot of noise.

In Summary

When it comes to setting long nets there are many variations on how to do it,

according to which part of the country you are in. The methods I have described are the ones that I find work best for me. I have tried others, including picking my net up loose without an anchor pin, and rolling the net on to a large pole so that it slides off the pole in clumps and is then spread out. All of these methods were no use to me, but were perfectly satisfactory to those who showed me the methods.

I know many people who do net who will scorn what I have written because it is not what they do – but that does not mean it is wrong. The secret is to find a method that suits your requirements.

CHAPTER 4

NETTING AT NIGHT

Now on to the important part, which is using your nets to catch live quarry, and how to go about doing it. There are three main ways in which a long net is used. The first and standard method is to use it at night to catch the rabbits as they run from their feeding grounds back towards home. The second method follows the same principle, but is used during the daytime when rabbits are perhaps feeding in woodland or are feeding in a crop that is being combined; as the field is cut, the rabbits will have to leave the crop and again head for home – only to find your nets blocking their path.

Finally it can be used as a stop net when ferreting, when it is used to snag the rabbits as they are bolted via the ferrets from their burrows.

Night netting is probably the method that most of you have read about and are keen to try. The principle mentioned above is quite simple, in that the nets are set between the rabbits and their home, and the rabbits are then driven back towards the nets. Needless to say, as with most things in life it is not as easy as it sounds, and good catches will only come with practice. Forget all the old stories you have heard in the pub of hauls of a hundred and more rabbits in one set of a long net – though perhaps they may indeed be true, especially if you are lucky enough to be talking to one of the 'old

school' rabbiters who can remember the days before myxomatosis.

Rabbiting has changed a great deal, as has the countryside, and to be able to catch a haul like that these days would be a great achievement. For night netting to be successful the rabbits need to be out feeding after dark, and then you must be able to set your nets up in the dark between the feeding rabbits and their burrows without startling them and causing them to head for home before your nets are in place. Therefore silence is a must, which is why I normally net alone. You also need to be sure that your ground is suitable for long netting.

If the fields are too small then it is likely that no matter how quiet you are, the rabbits will pick up on your presence and head for home. If you are lucky, the field will not be completely flat, and will have enough grass cover that even if they do become aware of you, they will duck down until they are run into the net; rabbits that do this are known as 'squatters'. To my mind, the best fields for netting are very rough, with clumps of nettles or brambles in the centre; the rabbits will often duck into this cover thinking they are safe.

Before you go out netting it is always best to assess the potential of your ground by going there in daytime, and seeing just how close you can get to the rabbits before they head for home. Use the contours of the land to your advantage. I net some very small fields but they are slightly rolling, and I can therefore approach the rabbits at an angle which means that I am not visible as they are grazing over the brow of the hill. I also cover some very large fields, but they are so open that I cannot net them because whichever way I try to approach my quarry I am clearly visible, even at night.

In a word, it is crucial that you understand the ground you are going to net. You will need to know where the burrows are, and what gates will allow you the easiest entry to the fields you intend to net: you must know your ground if you are going to have any success long netting. I find that the best sort of netting ground consists of medium-sized fields bordered by woods, hedges or ditches, thus offering the rabbiter some cover.

It is always worth checking that the landowner of the ground you are going to be using knows when you will be there, because the last thing you want is for your netting to be interrupted by the rather annoyed farmer who thinks he has poachers on his property. It is also worth carrying his written permission at all times, just in case you are challenged by a passing police officer or neighbour. I have found myself in this situation more than once, but the matter has been quickly dealt with when I have shown my signed letter to the concerned party.

Timing: When to Net

The actual time to net at night will vary according to the nature of the terrain you cover, and I believe it is something that you will only discover by researching your ground before you even start. Most of my long netting takes place during the winter months when the evenings and nights are longer, and also because there are not so many young rabbits at this time of year.

I have some areas where the rabbits never feed at night, preferring to feed early in the morning at dawn. These places are difficult to net as it is generally light when the rabbits are out feeding; however, that doesn't mean that it is impossible to net them, as you will discover when we discuss daytime netting.

The best areas are those where the rabbits come out to feed at dusk, and move further out to feed as the night wears on. Needless to say, the earlier you net, the more likely the rabbits are to be close to their burrows, so as a basic rule it is best to net at least a good couple of hours after dusk to ensure that the coney is a long way from home. There is no point in trying to catch rabbits that are only 10 or 20yd (9 or 18m) from their burrows, as they will be long gone as soon as you set foot in their field. Every area will be different: some rabbits on my ground come out as soon as it is dark and go far out into the field to feed; others will hover close to the burrows until three or four hours after dark. This is just another example of why you must study your quarry and your ground.

Finally you should consider how much time should be left between doing a set and returning to it. In my experience I have found that you need to leave at least a fortnight before returning to a set – though in actual fact, as you are only going to want to net on the darkest of nights and in the most suitable conditions, you will probably find that you end up returning to a set at intervals of three to four weeks, depending on how much ground you are working.

Do not visit a site too regularly, because the rabbits will become jumpy and will work out what you are up to, and you will soon find that netting is impossible.

Weather Conditions

The weather can be the netman's friend, and should be used to your advantage. The best nights are those with no moon and a breeze blowing in your favour. The wind is an important aspect to netting – in fact it is *the* most important aspect of netting, because if it is too strong it will make setting your nets difficult as they will continually blow down the runners and bunch up. I have had many nights when the wind is just so strong that no matter what I do the nets are impossible to set, and the slack/bag keeps blowing down the net and bunches around the peg, making it useless; then I will often tie my netting to the top and bottom runners to stop the slack spreading too much.

A light breeze is ideal, but you must use the wind to your favour and ensure that your scent is not blown towards the rabbits. I also find that nights with a little rain are good, and fog can also be good, providing it is not too thick; very often rabbits will not go out to feed in terrible weather. Avoid light nights, especially full moons, as this will be like daylight to the rabbits and you will not have a chance of setting your nets without being seen.

Livestock

Never net a field that contains livestock, because animals may well panic, and then they risk injuring you or themselves. You also run the risk of them hitting your nets, and cattle, for instance, will completely rip your nets to pieces. So avoid livestock at all costs!

The Set

This is the term used to describe the running out of a net or nets on a field, and the result that comes with it. For example, in a single night you may set nets over five different fields, and this would be counted as five sets.

The amount of netting you run out on a set will depend on the area and ground that you have to cover. Sometimes a hedge stretches 300yd (274m), but I know that the burrows are situated in just a small area of it, so I will net only the area in front of those burrows, because I know that is where the rabbits will make for. On other occasions I may have a ditch of 300yd that is riddled with burrows, and so I will net the whole length of the ditch, if I have enough nets, to ensure a good catch. It is easy to assume that all you have to do is run the net in a straight line along the area the rabbits will head for; but needless to say this is not the case, and there are several different styles of setting the net that are suitable for different situations.

The setting of the net needs to be done quickly but correctly to ensure that the rabbits are not aware of your presence: if you take too much time they will sense what is happening, even in the best conditions. On average I can now set about 300yd of net in around five or so minutes, whereas when I started this would have taken me a good forty minutes or more –

and setting nets at speed only comes with practice.

I don't know if there is a particular name for each type of set; I expect there are regional variances, as there is with many of the terms used with long netting. I have given the three types of set my own names, and I use these in the remainder of this chapter. I find that the most amount of netting in 4oz (113g) or 6oz (170g) nylon that I can carry comfortably on my own is 400yd (366m), and anything more than this is just too heavy – and in any case, it is very unusual for me to find a set that is over 400yd in one length; most of those I do seem to be around 150 (137m) to 300yd (274m).

The Straight Set

This is the most common situation that you will come across, and, as the name suggests, it is the set when you literally need to run the net in a straight line down the edge of a wood or hedge. The first thing to bear in mind is that you do not want to set the net too close to the edge of the area, as any loose twigs or brambles will tangle readily; therefore I set my nets about 5yd (4.6m) away from the edge of any cover.

The second thing that many do not think about is the fact that although most rabbits will make for the nets at speed, some will not, and as a result may actually run the length of the net and slip around behind it. The way to avoid this is to set your net out an angle at your start and finishing point, an arrangement I have always known as 'tailing', or 'edging' the net. This is a simple process of basically setting the last 5yd or so of the net at right angles towards the field, so that any rabbits that do try to run the net will become snagged.

You are probably wondering what to do if you are using more than one net, and how to join nets together to stop rabbits slipping through. Obviously you cannot just set your net, and then leave a gap and set another net, as rabbits will just dart through the gap. But again, joining

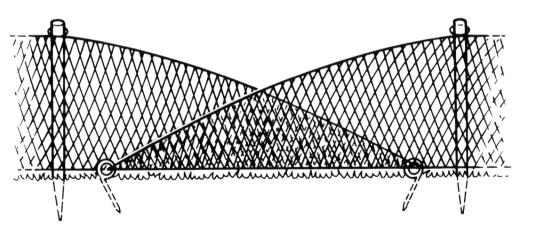

Two nets joined together by overlapping the first 5yd of the second net to the last 5yd of the first net so as to avoid any gaps that rabbits could pass through.

nets together when setting them is a very simple process. Once you have set your first net, place the anchor pin from your second net about 10yd along the first net and through its bottom runner. Then run the second net out, attaching it to the last peg you have put into the first net. By doing this the nets will overlap, and rabbits will not be able to slip through any gaps.

The amount of netting you run out on a straight set will depend on how many rabbits you hope to catch; so if the hedge is 500yd long and you only set 50yd of netting, you stand little chance of catching many rabbits unless you are lucky enough to get them to run directly into the one area you have covered. Ideally with a straight set you should net all of

the area the rabbits are likely to head for – the exception being if you only wanted to catch rabbits on a particular part of the field. This leads us nicely on to the second style of set.

The Part Straight Set

As already mentioned, you would use this set when rabbits inhabit only a small area of a hedge or wood, or if you only wanted to catch them on part of a field. You would set your net in front of the home area, but instead of tailing the net, it will be set in a slight semi-circle. You want the net to be set so that all the home area is covered, and ideally at least 20 to 30yd (18 to 27m) on either side. By doing this, when you run the rabbits towards

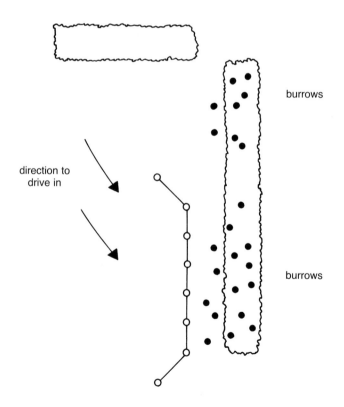

direction to drive in

burrows

burrows

A part straight set net.

home, as they get closer they will start to bunch up and run into the semi-circle.

The Corner Set

This set is used when the rabbits are likely to make for a gateway in the corner of two fields, or, as is often the case, their burrows are situated along two hedge lines that run off at right angles. It is a set that may be used on its own or as part of a straight set. The idea is that you will set the net again in a semi-circle from the corner and down both lengths of hedge line for between 30 and 50yd. You would then drive the rabbits towards the corner area from the far side of the feeding area. No tail is used with this sort of set, as the net effectively tails itself.

Running the Rabbits Home

As with any set, you need to push the rabbits towards the netting you have set in place, and this can be done in a number of ways. Again, this is where research comes in, because you will see by the rabbits' runs which way they tend to travel. You need to ensure that the wind is in your favour, since you will have set your nets with your scent blowing away from the rabbits. You now need to get behind them and send them towards home.

If you go crashing into the middle of the field from the direction you have just netted, all you will do is scatter the coneys in the opposite direction, the one that is not netted, and your time will be

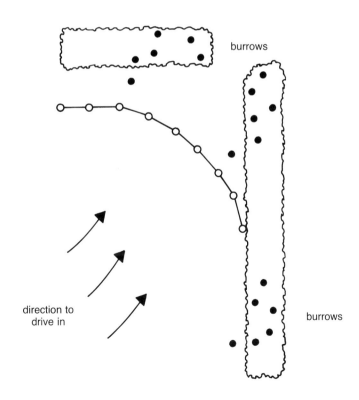

A corner set net.

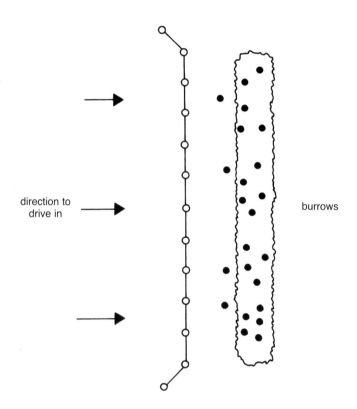

A straight set net.

direction to drive in →

burrows

completely wasted. You need to creep behind your quarry with the wind in your favour, and then flush them towards your nets. My chosen method of doing this is to shake a small tin filled with stones, and to whistle, which in most cases scatters the rabbits well towards home. Some people opt to take a bright torch with them, and to shine this at the sitting rabbits; however, I find this spooks them too much for future trips and is best avoided. If a torch *is* needed I would suggest using a small headlamp because this will leave your hands free and will have a very low beam; but even this should be used as a very last resort, perhaps to untangle the net in extreme circumstances.

The Running Cord

One method that is open to the two-man team is that of the running cord; it is ideal for areas where the rabbits often sit tight and refuse to budge. It basically consists of a reel of cord, with one man holding the reeled end and the other the loose end. The two people operating the running cord are behind the rabbits, and run the cord out the entire length of the field in which they intend to run the rabbits home. When the second man has reached the position he requires he will signal to the other by a short whistle or a double tug of the cord. Both men will then walk towards the net with the cord held between them.

As they walk, the cord touches the rabbits and the contact makes them up and run for home. This is a good method, but because I work alone it is not one that I often use. Again, it is best suited to smooth ground, and the cord has to be sturdy in order to withstand being dragged and to make the rabbits move effectively. In some cases, for example fields that are covered with thistles or similar, the 'running cord' may not be practical, and in such a situation the first method is often the best, providing that you zigzag the field as you go.

Despatching your Quarry

After running in the field and reaching your net, your next job is to quickly and humanely despatch your quarry. By far the easiest method of doing this when netting at night is to strike the rabbit hard on the head with a priest. Once all the rabbits are despatched, I can then set about removing them from the nets. You must ensure that your rabbits are despatched humanely so that any suffering is kept to a minimum. If using a priest is not to your liking, other methods

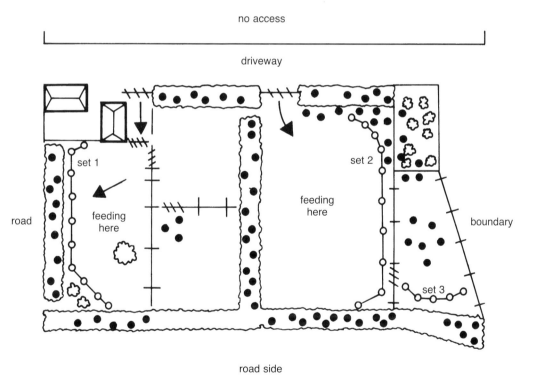

The authors netting plan he uses on a smallholding; this plan allows the author to net three sets in the course of a night – providing, of course, that the wind is right.

A bagged rabbit, showing once again the importance of the bag in the net.

Rabbits hung up to keep cool and out of predators' way. (Always ensure you do not hang them by a footpath or bridleway.)

are suitable, such as the rabbit chop or chinning.

Quite apart from the angle of suffering caused, any rabbits left undespatched may start to scream, and this sound will alert any other rabbits on neighbouring sets to the danger. Once removed from the net, the rabbits should be hung by the leg out of harm's way for collection later on; if left lying on the ground you may well find that Mr Fox will carry off your catch.

Unwanted Visitors

From time to time you may catch other quarry apart from rabbits in your nets. For instance, should a deer hit a long net it will generally rip through it and make good its escape. By far the most troublesome visitors, however, are the fox and badger: both are a nightmare to remove, and both can deliver a terrible bite. You may have permission to cull foxes, in which case your problem is easily solved. I always carry a heavy thumb-stick in addition to a priest to assist me with such a problem.

Badgers are a different matter since they are a protected species, and as such every effort should be made to free one quickly if it is caught. The thumb-stick comes in useful again here, as it can be used to hold Brock still while you carefully cut away the netting or unsnare him from your net. Badgers seldom get entangled, and due to their size, even when they do hit a net, are often large enough to free themselves.

Hedgehogs will occasionally get caught and should be freed, which again may end up with you cutting the net. By far the worst offender, however, is the domestic cat. If caught up, these work themselves into a frenzy of claw and teeth, and are the devil to remove. Again, a trusty thumb-stick will help to hold one still while you cut it free. As you have probably gathered there are times when your nets will need repair, so it is also a good idea to know the basics of net-making to enable you to do this.

Picking up

Once your set is complete you need to pick up your nets and return them to your chosen carrying method. On returning home they will need to be dried out, and once this has been done they will need to be run out in daylight over a suitable location so that any holes and tears can be repaired. To dry nets, by far the easiest way in the standard modern house is to place the net in the airing cupboard for a few hours. An alternative to this, and especially in the summer, is to leave the net balled up but slightly spread on the washing line and to let the sun do its work. You should also check your pegs to see if any of them have suffered any damage; I often find hazel pegs that have been directly hit by a rabbit and have slightly cracked and thus need replacing.

We will deal with the care of the quarry later, but needless to say, on returning home it should be stored in a cool location prior to being skinned and gutted. If you intend to sell your catch you need to ensure it is in a good condition, and even if it is being stored for no more than a few hours before the game dealer's opens, you must keep it dry and clear of flies, which could perish your hard-earned catch of rabbits.

CHAPTER 5

DAYTIME EXCURSIONS

Daytime netting follows many of the same principles as night netting; I often net by day, and generally it deals with rabbits that are living in relatively thick cover. In addition I will often net areas during the early morning and evening where rabbits feed in the daytime. These habitats are often orchards or thick woodland where the rabbits feel so secure that they live above ground and do not use burrows. Gorse is also popular cover for rabbits, as are areas dotted with large rocks under which they can seek shelter.

Dealing with Woodland

Should you have to deal with a population of rabbits inhabiting scrub or woodland, your job will be made easier if it has natural gaps or rides through it. Then it is a simple case of setting your nets in these areas and splitting the woodland up into blocks; these are then flushed through, and the rabbits will head in the direction they are being pushed towards – which is where your nets are set.

If the cover is very thick the rabbits will be hard to move, so you may need a good dog and a team of beaters to flush the area through effectively. I often work a bank of about 500yd (460m) of thick scrub, netting it with 50yd (46m) nets at intervals along the hillside it is situated

on; I then work through the cover with the dogs, and often come away with a dozen or so rabbits. This scrub is only about 30yd (27m) wide, but it is very thick; for various reasons it cannot be shot or snared, so netting in this manner is ideal.

Larger blocks of woodland can be dealt with in the same way, but needless to say, the bigger the wood, the more net is needed, and the more people to flush the cover through. In some cases there may be rabbit burrows situated in the woodland, and any sensible, thinking rabbit will make straight for these. One way to avoid this is to stink out the burrows a day before netting so that the rabbits stay above ground. This can, however, prove a mammoth task, and is something that I would not recommend the sporting netsman to get too excited about. I tend not to net large blocks of woodland, and prefer to keep to small clumps of gorse or blackthorn that I know will always hold a few rabbits.

Often in conjunction with the net I will carry a gun to shoot any rabbits that go the wrong way, and treat these sorts of trip as pot-hunting excursions as much as anything else. The only time I have netted large areas is when I have been requested to do so, on a driven vermin shoot. This type of netting has proved very successful, especially when the rabbits have been

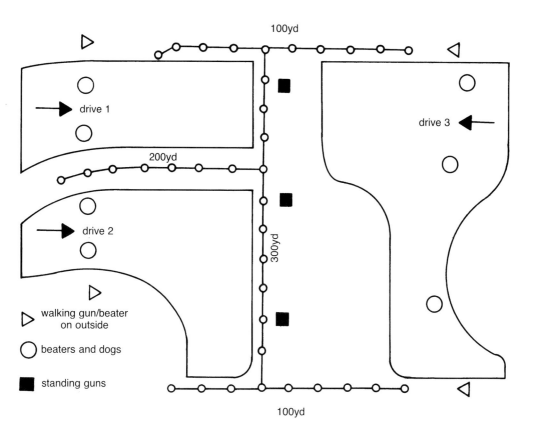

100yd

drive 1

200yd

drive 2

drive 3

300yd

▷ walking gun/beater
on outside

◯ beaters and dogs

■ standing guns

100yd

Netting on a large scale around woodland. This can be a time-consuming task.

above ground, when their burrows were flooded out by heavy rain.

Netting Orchards and Crops

By far my favourite method of netting during the daytime is when dealing with orchard areas and crops. Needless to say, netting crops is often done in the summer as a form of pest control, and the netter has the advantage over the shooting man as he can release any milky or pregnant rabbits should he need to.

There are two ways that I net crops in the daytime: the first is in amongst light crops such as hay, high enough for the rabbits to get into without them seeing me, but not so thick that I cannot flush them out. As with night netting, the nets are set between the rabbits and their home, and the rabbits are driven towards the nets from the crops they are feeding in. As a rule this is best done at dawn or dusk when they seem to be feeding the most avidly. Obviously you will have to walk through the crop to get the rabbits out, so ensure that the landowner is happy with this, and that you are not going to do more damage than the grazing rabbits!

The second method involves netting a crop that is being cut, and again you net the rabbits' home area. As the crop gets smaller the rabbits will start to break cover and run for home, and en route they hit the net; my best catch in this manner was fifty-three from a 10-acre beanfield. I often use this method in conjunction with my lurcher, whom I use to run any rabbits that go in the wrong direction.

Netting orchards is again similar to netting crops. As a rule the rabbits' burrows will be in the surrounding hedges, so these areas are netted and the orchard is then run through, and any rabbits feeding within the orchard will be caught as they make for home.

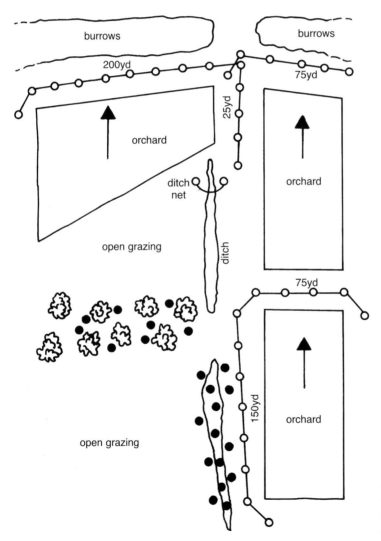

Netting around a mix of orchards and scrubland, mainly bramble and gorse.

Netting around typical downland cover of mixed scrub.

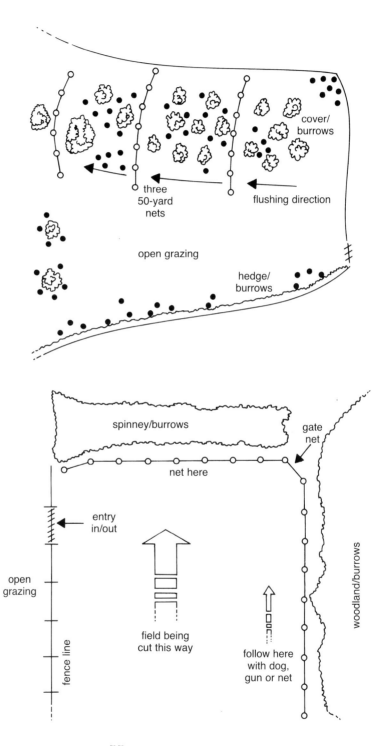

cover/ burrows

three 50-yard nets

flushing direction

open grazing

hedge/ burrows

spinney/burrows

gate net

net here

entry in/out

open grazing

fence line

field being cut this way

follow here with dog, gun or net

woodland/burrows

Netting around crops that are being cut.

Gaps like the one in the hedge shown above can prove an excellent opportunity for the netsman to run a net out.

Ferrets and Long Nets

The final use of a long net in the daytime is as a stop net when ferreting. The net is set around the rabbits' burrow, and the rabbits are flushed from the burrow into the net. It is an ideal method to use on burrows situated in bramble or thick cover which are not practical to purse net.

Long nets can also be used on large burrows in conjunction with purse nets. I often use long nets when ferreting to cover both of the above, and also when ferreting hedge lines that I cannot access to set purse nets. I set my long nets at either end of the hedge line, and in most cases the rabbits will run the length of the hedge and become tangled. This does not always go to plan, and sometimes I lose more than I should; however, I am lucky to have a good dog, who claims his share that run wide of the nets.

One thing to bear in mind when long netting with ferrets is that you will often

Netting around a large burrow. Nets are also set across the burrow to divide it into workable quarters. Purse nets are then set at intervals to stop rabbits running from hole to hole.

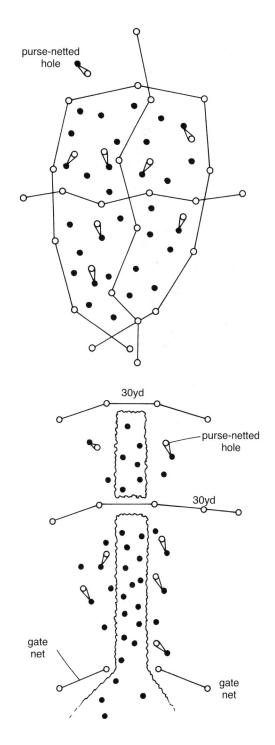

purse-netted hole

30yd

purse-netted hole

30yd

gate net

gate net

Netting a hedge line when ferreting. This method is ideal if combined with a good dog or possibly a standing gun.

The author ferreting around some burrows with a long net in the late summer.

find on large burrows – and especially open ones – that rabbits will come to the hole very cautiously before bolting. For this reason it is well worth setting a few purse nets to deal with any rabbits that may make a short dash from one hole to another. On very large warrens my method of choice is to surround the warren with a long net or two, and then to net across the warren with long nets to divide the warren into four sections. Every fourth hole is then purse netted to account for any rabbits trying to slip back in when they bolt, and I find this a very effective way of ensuring that not too many rabbits slip back into the warren eventually causing the ferret to lie up and a dig for the ferreter!

When setting a net around a burrow, you will find that the meshes tend to bunch up, and that the runners will sometimes pull short, especially if the net is being set in a circular fashion. To overcome this you may have to hitch the net more than you would normally; it can also be a good idea on any circular bends to add a second peg at a right-angle to give a little extra support. This peg will not hold the net, but will be positioned behind the peg holding the net to support it.

I will avoid the temptation of writing more about the practice of ferreting, because if I did, this book would soon escalate to gigantic proportions and the subjects at hand be overshadowed. Suffice it to say that for me, ferreting has to be one of the most exciting and interesting ways of catching rabbits. Like long netting, it takes time to learn how to ferret properly – and it also takes ferrets time to learn the skill of bolting rabbits. The benefit compared to long netting is that there is a huge range of ferreting books on the market, and it is very easy to get advice and information on the subject.

A ferret comes out from the ground after a short dig.

CHAPTER 6

OTHER TYPES OF LONG NET

As you have probably become aware, there are some situations when the standard long net is not really going to be that suitable. You may also find that you simply cannot get to grips with the standard system, and no matter what, become completely tangled in your own net. Do not fear: all is not lost. There are several alternatives to the standard style of long netting on which we have concentrated, and you may find that these are more suitable to your needs.

The Drop Net

The first thing we shall look at is the situation where the fields that you have to work are too small for you to set a long net in the normal manner without alerting every rabbit in the county. If this is your problem, then the drop-net system could be for you. The drop-netting system varies from county to county but is a very simple idea. The net is set, but is suspended above the ground on a large sliding rod system, allowing rabbits to pass under it. When your chosen night comes, you drop the net that will then slide to the ground between the rabbits and home, and you then run the rabbits home as per normal – the only difference being

that you have set the net up in advance of the night's netting.

To explain this more clearly I must first describe the rod system that holds the net in place. My own system consists of a thick (1.5in) broom handle measuring 5ft (1.5m) in length. It has a hole drilled in it about 20in (50cm) from the top: this hole is used to hold a pin that supports the slider that will hold the net. The slider is a piece of metal with two steel rings fitted to the back of it, which fit over the broom handle. The front of the slider has a grommet, which is in place to attach the net's top and bottom draw cords. These grommets are attached 1in (2.5cm) from the top and 1in from the bottom of the metal slider.

The poles and sliders replace the net pegs, so, as with a standard net, you will need one pole and slider to every 5yd (4.6m) or so of net. The net will be set attached to the sliders, which, as we have mentioned, will be raised on the pole support so that rabbits can pass with ease underneath the netting. The pins that hold the sliders in place will have a cord run through them, and this cord is pulled to a location some distance away, that you will be able to access without alerting the rabbits. The maximum distance this seems to work at effectively is 100yd

(91m). When the night comes to drop the net, you make your way to the cord, and by pulling it, the pins holding the sliders are released, causing the net and sliders to drop to the ground and hopefully block the rabbit's path.

Although this may sound like an ideal method, there are several things you need to consider. Firstly, I find that a net of no more than 100yd (91m) can be effectively used when drop netting. Anything larger than this is simply too difficult to drop, and trying to get it to fall correctly is almost impossible to do with any effect. Secondly, you need to ensure that you can get the drop cord to a location where you can reach it without being seen. Finally, the biggest problem is setting the net in advance in a location where it will not be disturbed or damaged by nosy passers-by.

Areas where livestock are located are no good for netting, as are locations by footpaths or bridleways, as it would only take one vandal to destroy your net. This means that using a drop net can be quite

A drop-net system used by the author consisting of a broom-handle support and a drainpipe slider.

The author's current drop-net system consisting of a metal slider hand-made by a friend; the support pin is a metal rod with a nut welded to it.

limited opportunity. I tend to use mine in garden areas that are well out of the public eye, and have the added bonus that the property owner will often be able to keep an eye on the net when you are not about.

As well as livestock you should also consider wildlife when drop netting. There is no point setting the net in an area where it is obvious that deer are regular visitors, as there is a potential risk that when the net is raised, a deer could hit it when trying to jump the fence or hedge along which the net is set.

There is, of course, more than one way to drop net, and you may find that a different method to the one I have described could well be more suitable for your needs. Take, for example, a situation where perhaps rabbits are feeding out on a certain area in the afternoon. These rabbits may be feeding in an orchard in front of the hedge, and by setting the net on the drop-net system, or by simply using a normal pegged system and hooking the bottom runner up but without running the cord, you may save yourself time if you intend to drop the net a few hours later by simply walking the length of the net and removing the pins or dropping the bottom runner as you go.

By using this method it is quite practical to set up more than one net in the raised position, because you are not going to use the running cord to drop the net. I often use this method in the summer when I know that whatever the weather, some rabbits will be found feeding out in the area I intend to net.

If you are going to set up a drop net, even for a few hours, always ensure the landowner is aware of where you are putting it so that any possible disturbance of the rabbits is avoided.

Alternative Drop-Netting Systems

If you don't fancy the described method of drop netting, two alternatives I once used could well be suitable for you. As described above, the first was simply to hook the bottom runner on to the top of each peg, and then to drop the net when I was ready to. The second method was just as simple, and entailed a clothes peg being tied to each peg. The clothes pegs were tied so the teeth were facing upwards; the bottom runner could then be clamped in the peg and removed for dropping.

Undoubtedly there will be several netters reading this who have their own methods, all of which are successful, so you may find a method that is even more suitable than mine. That, to me, is one of the joys of long netting, as every one who nets will have their own variations as to how they do it, which to me adds to the fun.

Permanent-Set and Pre-Set Long Nets

The final types of long net that need to be mentioned are the permanent-set net and the pre-set or tied-set long net. Firstly, the permanent-set net is a long net that is attached to its pegs permanently, and is picked up and run out with the pegs still attached to it. This sort of net has no anchor pins, and the net is attached to a starting and finishing peg and then has the rest of the pegs attached at regular intervals. The pegs are generally held in place by a very strong rubber band, though in some cases the draw cord is sewn around each peg.

the cord is permanently
banded to the top of the
peg and the pegs are
always attached to the net

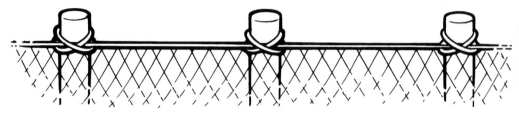

An example of a net with the pegs permanently attached to the runners.

the net meshes are tied to
the cord at regular
intervals and the slack
netting is fixed in place

the cord is hitched to the
top of the peg and can
be removed from the peg

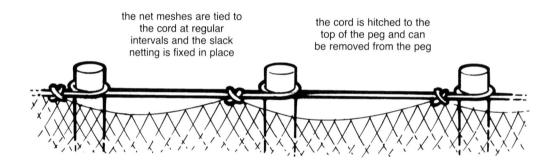

An example of a pre-set net; the knot indicates the points where the netting is tied to the runners.

the net meshes are not
tied to the runner/cord and
can be manually spread

the cord is hitched to the
top of the peg and can
be removed from the peg

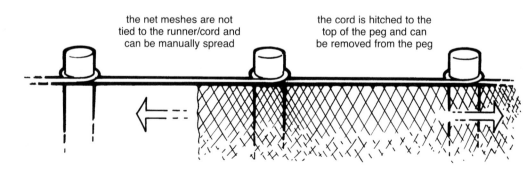

A standard set net with the runners not tied to the net or the pegs.

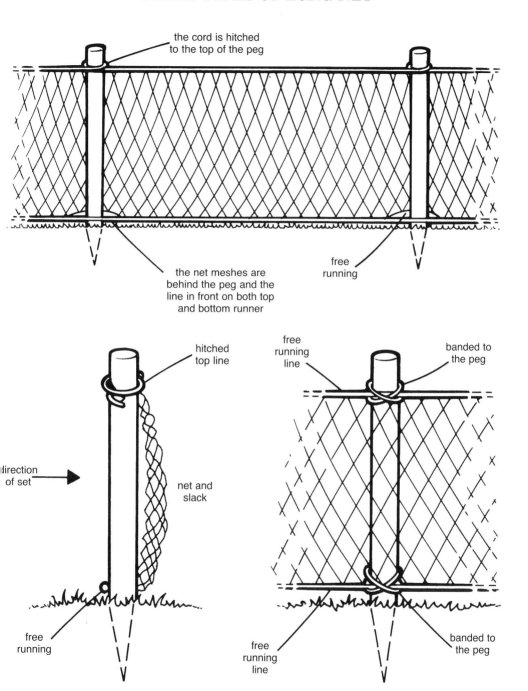

the cord is hitched
to the top of the peg

the net meshes are
behind the peg and the
line in front on both top
and bottom runner

free
running

hitched
top line

free
running
line

banded to
the peg

direction
of set

net and
slack

free
running

free
running
line

banded to
the peg

*An example of a net that has been permanently set to the top and bottom
runners.*

This sort of netting system will generally be incorporated with some sort of carrying device to hold it nicely in place when travelling to and from the hunting field. As with drop netting, I am sure there are several variations to this sort of style of netting. I believe that the most popular system – and the only complete set system that I have seen on the market – is the quick-set long-net system as sold by Brian and Liam Brinded. This incorporates a net set on to its pegs, which is carried in a unique basket-style carrier; and from what I have seen, it is extremely popular.

To be honest, I am not a great supporter of permanent-set systems, because whenever I have tried them, I end up getting the net snagged on the pegs and in a terrible mess. However, I do own a couple of permanent-set nets, and do from time to time venture out with them, and do get some success: this, however, is usually when ferreting, as I still prefer the traditional style of long netting when going out at night. I am not in any way trying to fault the permanent-set net: it is certainly very popular, but it is just not the system for me. Indeed, it is true to say that I know of many who use permanent-set netting systems, and use them all the time when ferreting and indeed at night and do swear by them and the fact that they are easy to set in seconds. Part of my

Without the net tied in, the netting can easily slide along the runners and become bunched up.

problem could be that I have always made my own permanent-set systems that are probably not as good operationally as a professionally made system.

In conclusion, if you fancy giving the permanent-net system a go, why not pick one up and try it? After all, if it's not for you, it is not going to be the end of the world. The permanent-set style of net seems to be very popular at the moment, and is certainly here to stay; and from what I have seen, many of the professional rabbit catchers have developed some kind of permanent-set type of net to meet their individual requirements. The key seems to be that everyone has a different system that they swear by, and I feel it really is a case of finding out what works best for you should you wish to net using this system of netting.

The pre-set net is different altogether, and is something that I would strongly recommend to the beginner. It simply means that at intervals – generally every 5yd (4.6m) or so – the netting is tied on to the top and bottom draw cords of the nets and thus cannot slide the whole length of the net and become tangled. Most of my nets are pre-set in this manner, and it really does make life a lot easier, especially when it is a little windier than you first expected. Needless to say, the advantages of this speak for themselves, and can save the novice a lot of time and effort trying to untangle a massed ball of netting that has slid to a point on the net and then got caught around a piece of bramble or old wire.

Trammel Nets

Trammel long nets are a type of net that I have tried, but I have never really seen any great advantage in them, although they certainly are good fun to use for a change once in a while. My long nets, both the ones I have bought and the ones I have made, are made of diamond meshing, by which it simply means that the meshes are formed in a diamond shape. It is, however, possible to make netting into a square mesh, although I have not covered this, because I really find that diamond meshing is the best to use and the easiest to knit.

The only time that square mesh really comes into play is on a trammel long net. The difference to this and a standard net is that your standard net is attached to a second wall of netting. This will be square-meshed netting of a much larger mesh size, normally 6 to 9sq in (39 to 58sq cm – this is the size I have always used on my trammel nets).

This wall of netting does not contain any slack netting, and your standard net is permanently set to the wall of meshing at intervals, ensuring of course that the bag is well spread. The idea is that, when the rabbits hit the net, the standard netting pulls through one of the larger squares and thus enmeshes the rabbit within each larger square, supposedly making it harder for them to escape. As mentioned, I have tried this, but cannot really say that I notice any huge difference for the effort involved in attaching the second wall of netting. I would suggest that if you fancy trying it, do so on a small net when ferreting and see how you find its performance.

The trammel long net is not a new idea, and was probably one of the first types of long net used, as in their original status long nets were probably simply adapted fishing nets used to take game.

CHAPTER 7

THE LONG-NETTER'S DOG

Let us assume and hope that you now have a basic knowledge of how to set a long net and use it in the field with reasonable success. Your thoughts may now turn to the prospect of getting a dog to help you with your task, or indeed you may already have a dog that you wish to use for this purpose.

Firstly, beware of anyone who offers you a trained dog for long netting, because if such a dog exists I can assure you the owner would not want to part with it for either love or money. It is my view that when it comes to ferreting and shooting, with time and the correct training, almost any dog can be taught to work steadily with ferrets, and to hunt rabbits effectively – I have seen spaniels and even Alsatians work well to ferrets. However, I do know how much effort has to be put into training a ferreting dog, and I am not trying to make its role seem easy. I am not the world's best trainer, largely because I have no patience; nevertheless I have successfully trained various dogs for ferreting and general rabbiting, and once had a very good long-netting dog, although this was probably due more to the intelligence of the dog rather than anything that I did. In brief, anyone who ferrets will know that a good dog for ferreting will mark a burrow, and will not, under any circumstances, snap at the ferrets.

Some people train their dogs not to take rabbits caught in nets, whilst others teach them to hold a rabbit in the net until they can get to it and despatch the rabbit. I have always favoured the second method, as I often work alone and find it makes my life a lot easier. I will not even attempt to offer training advice since I am not at all good at it, as I have already pointed out; nevertheless, I will describe the features that, in my own humble opinion, a good long-netting dog should display.

To do this I will digress, and relate the story of the only dog that I have ever had that was successful at long netting. Ringer came to me when I left home for the first time, and arrived by accident, rather than by design. My wife and I visited a rescue centre, and I had my heart set on leaving with a lurcher as I had always yearned for a good strong running dog to keep me company in the field. But whilst walking round we were suddenly confronted by a small Collie × Labrador who looked at us with large woeful eyes within her kennel. My wife fell in love with her, and two days later after a diversity of paperwork was completed, we picked up our nine-month-old bitch and took her home.

Things did not go smoothly, and she went on to destroy our sofa and various other household items and was almost

The author's lurcher marking a burrow.

sent back; but we stuck with her, and things slowly improved. Like all Collie crosses she was very clever, and I held out that she might be suitable for working – and this did prove to be the case. I stumbled my way through training her, and somehow, after she had turned two years old, I had a relatively good rough shooting and ferreting dog who was extremely loyal and lived to work.

Ferreting was her passion, and she was an amazing dog for this task. When she was five she would, on many an occasion, sit by a hole and then pluck the rabbit out as it stuck its head out. I also used her for retrieving when pigeon shooting, and for flushing rabbits when walking through cover. On many an occasion she caught foxes and rabbits when lamping, and although she did not have the speed of a lurcher or long dog, she would follow the beam and snatch her catch with a great amount of cunning.

Her long-netting experience came purely by accident. I would often use long nets when ferreting, and became aware that she never ran into the net but would always jump it. This was also the case when netting blocks of cover during the daytime, and I decided to give her a try at some netting at night. As I have said, I am somewhat of a loner so often go netting on my own, and it struck me that if I could get her to run the field in to the nets, it would leave me free to stay by the net and despatch any rabbits that hit it. So I set about teaching her how to work at night with long nets – or more to the point, allowing her to show me she could do it.

The first few runs out were for practice purposes, and I would keep her with me whilst setting the nets; then I would head off into the dark and zigzag the field towards the nets with her still with me. My main concern was that, because I had used her to course rabbits, she might well have taken to pursuing one rabbit, rather than flushing the field in, and would be of no use in the netting field. This was something I did not need to worry about, because using her brain, she soon learnt that if the nets were set, it was simply a case of flushing the rabbits and not

chasing them, just as she did when netting in the daytime.

All this did not happen overnight, and it took a good year for her to master what was required; but we got to the point where I would simply leave her sitting by the end of the net, and once it was set would signal her to run round behind the rabbits and flush them for home. We had many a good night, and in all honesty it was her workability that really got me hooked on netting at night regularly.

Sadly all good things have to end, and it was the hardest moment in my life when at six-and-a-half years I had to send her back to the rescue centre. Unfortunately she was unreliable with children, and I have three, who came along after the dog. We worked hard to build a bond between her and the children, but one day she went for my youngest for no reason, and even *I* had to admit that we could no longer keep her. Kennelling was not an option because we didn't have the space, and re-homing was the only answer, short of the dog and I being kicked out of the house. She was re-homed to a couple and is doing well, but I still miss her and think of her daily. I am of the belief that if you commit to a dog you should keep it, and have no time for the dog-swapping fraternity; so having to part with her really broke my heart, but it had to be done.

Breed and Required Character Traits

With regard to long netting, you need to ensure, as with Ringer, that firstly, your dog will not run into the nets, and secondly, that it will not chase its quarry but will flush it towards the netted area. It is

Dogs used for long netting must learn to jump the long net.

ideal if the dog will sit by the end of the net whilst you set it up, but it is imperative that it is silent, since if it barks or yaps it will obviously defeat the purpose, and any rabbits will be home before you have started.

The breed of dog for such a purpose should be seriously considered. Steady-mannered dogs are the most suitable, and the few good dogs I have come across have tended to have Collie or Labrador origins. The standard rabbiting dogs are the lurcher and terrier, although in my opinion these types are the worst to train for long netting, since by the nature of their job they are often used to chase rabbits rather than to flush them.

My current charge is a monster of a lurcher – or a 'long dog', as some would call it – a Greyhound × Deerhound. If you know your lurchers you are probably now wondering why someone would have such a cross, when their main quarry is rabbit. The answer is simply that it is a cross I have always liked, and although it is more commonly a type of lurcher used for coursing – which I do not indulge in – my current dog, who at $2^1/_2$ years old is still learning, is already a good ferreting dog and even accompanies me rough shooting.

When it comes to long netting, however, he is at present close to useless, and I am keen to see how he gets on over the next year, as in my limited knowledge of dog training it is between two and three years that a dog really masters its trade and shows potential. When using nets in the daytime he is very careful not to hit them, and in fact never has. The problem is that I also run him at night on rabbits, when he does as he has been taught to do in the daytime, namely he chases a rabbit rather than just goes round the field flushing them.

My main aim will be to produce a smaller breed, I hope with some Collie in it to produce a slightly more intelligent lurcher, and one a little shorter in the leg, which will take to long netting.

From what I have seen there are very few good quality long-netting dogs left these days, mainly due to the fact that there are very few long netters! With this in mind, if you are intent on using a dog for netting, at the very least ensure that it will not collide with the nets and damage itself, and also that it has had a thorough training in basic obedience: as with any type of working dog, it is imperative that basic obedience is established first before trying to run the dog in the field. Again, this is something I have often omitted to do because I have been in such a mad rush to get a dog working – indeed, it is something I am guilty of with my current lurcher.

I have had to go backwards in his training to ensure that the basics of sitting and staying are maintained, because without these basics I strongly believe that any dog will perform badly in the field. What good is a gun dog that rushes into a kill and will not return if it cannot find its quarry? Likewise, what good is a lurcher or long dog that simply runs on its quarry with no intention of returning until it catches? Whatever dog I have, I always ensure that it comes when called or to a whistle, no matter how intent it is on what it is doing. Again, without this basic training a dog used for long netting is likely just to run on one rabbit and end up in a heap in the net, damaging the net or itself, or both.

In conclusion, only use a dog you are sure will be up to the task, and if in doubt, work without it.

CHAPTER 8

OTHER NETS

Long nets aside, there are three other types of net that the netsman can, and should, take advantage of in the field. The first of these is the purse net, which we have briefly mentioned. The second is the ditch or hedge net, which in simple terms and in most parts of the country is a large-sized purse net with numerous uses when ferreting or on general trips out. Finally there is the gate net, which apart from its set use as suggested by its name, can serve many other purposes if you have the inclination to try.

The Purse Net

Firstly let us look at the widely used purse net. Anyone who has ferrets or has been ferreting will know of this net. In simple terms and for the non-ferreter, it consists of a net usually between 3ft and 4ft (0.9 and 1.2m) in length, and about 2ft (0.6m) wide. The net is attached to a ring or slider on each end, and running around the net and through the slider/ring is a draw cord, held securely by a good strong peg. How it works when ferreting is that the purse net is set over a rabbit hole, and the rabbit bolts from the hole into the net, which when hit by the rabbit slides down the draw cord and enmeshes the rabbit! As always, in practice it is not quite as simple as this, and I am always trying –

as are most ferreters – to find the perfect net that will hold a rabbit tight and not snag on brambles or twigs.

The standard English purse net is always set on a ring as opposed to a slider. Generally the ring is welded set, and 1in (2.5cm) in diameter. The net via the draw cord is then held in place by a peg that is pushed firmly in above the set area. The French equivalent is known as a 'bourse' net, and instead of a ring has a slider at the top and bottom. This serves the same purpose as the ring, but the big difference is that the bourse net has a peg attaching it at the top and bottom. This works really well, because when a rabbit hits the net it cannot push the bottom of the net out, and thus has much less chance of escaping. As a result I use nets that combine both and have rings on each end, but are also attached with a peg at top and bottom.

The top peg is the securing peg, and in my case these are usually cut from a piece of hazel (normally the leftovers from my long-net pegs). The bottom peg is there as a support, and either I use a thinner piece of hazel, or a strong piece of short fencing wire that can easily be pushed into the ground in any conditions. Different people use different types of peg; I know of some who use long blunted nails because the ground they work is very hard. There are various options available when it comes to choosing a peg, and it is up to the user to find the best for their needs, metal, plastic or wood pegs all serving the same purpose.

The size of the net is the most important factor, because if it is not big enough in width and length there will not be enough room for a rabbit to get properly balled up. Next to the net's actual size, the size of the meshes is also important. Most standard purse nets come in 2in (5cm) mesh size, although I prefer a mesh of $2^1/_8$in (5.4cm), as I do with my long nets; again this may seem picky, but it does make a difference. I find that $2^1/_4$in (5.6cm) mesh sizes on purse nets can be too big, depending on the material used to make the net. Thus if the net is made from nylon, it will stretch with use, so a $2^1/_4$in mesh can soon become a $2^1/_2$in (6.3in) mesh size, which is too big and will allow rabbits to pass through.

A correctly set purse net; note the draw cord running around the outside of the net and the rabbit hole.

Hemp or spun nylon will not stretch as much, but I find when knitting with it that it seems to make larger meshes anyway with the pull in it, so a $2^1/_8$in (5.4cm) mesh is ideal. Given the above, I opt to use nets made to a length of 4.5ft (1.35m), with $2^1/_8$in meshes. These are knitted to a width of fourteen to eighteen meshes across, which is about two and a bit, to $2^1/_2$ft (0.75m) in width.

As with bought long nets, the same applies to purse nets in that the cheapest can be purchased in nylon generally from 3oz or 4oz. These are all right, but they tangle easily on brambles and twigs, and are, in my opinion, a confounded nuisance to everyone except the ferreter who has the luxury of working completely open burrows. I would recommend nets in three materials commercially: these are spun nylon, hemp and the thicker nylon available in 10oz or 12oz. All of these are readily available from most suppliers at a variety of prices, and as with long nets the same pros and cons apply with the materials.

To the netter who intends to make his or her own purse net, I would also suggest three other mediums that can be used: first of all there is garden jute/twine, which is similar to hemp but is a lot cheaper to buy; however, I would stress that it comes in a variety of qualities (this is something we will look at when we discuss net-making). The other two mediums are cotton cord, which has the same issues as jute; and a twine that I am informed is called Rylon or Rayon (this is the only name I have been given for it), and I believe is a nylon/cotton mix. Rylon is my favourite medium when I am lucky enough to get it, as it seems to be indestructible, and available in many mediums at a very reasonable cost; the

drawback, however, is finding it, as it is not easily obtained!

Finally I would advise not to use a mesh of under 2in (5cm), because I can assure you, after learning from my own mistakes, that meshes smaller than this are two small and will cost you dearly in rabbits; I would rather lose a few small rabbits than a lot of larger ones by using small mesh sizes that most rabbits will be able to bounce off. I once made the mistake of making a spun-nylon long net for someone, and produced it in mesh of $1^1/_2$in (3.7cm) instead of the requested $2^1/_4$in (5.6cm) mesh size. This net was quickly returned and was next to useless in the field for any purpose except as a stop net – and even then it was not the greatest; so when I say I learned the hard way, I really did, because this cost me dearly in time and materials as I had to remake the net to the correct size.

The purse net is the ferreter's tool and weapon, but do not just put it by for ferreting. I mainly use long nets for ferreting, with a few purse nets set between the nets to apprehend any rabbits trying to dive from hole to hole. This is because I mainly ferret alone, and it can take a lot of time to set up purse nets because I ferret a lot of thick cover. The long net is an easier choice for me as I can set these around the burrows and just net any open holes with purse nets.

Using solely purse nets could be the best option for a gang, or for the ferreter who doesn't have a dog. I have only really turned to long nets for ferreting, rather than purses, in the past decade; before this I had no dog, so opted for purse nets more frequently. Having a good dog when ferreting really does pay dividends, because instead of spending hours clearing any cover from a burrow so as to set purse nets, I now use my dog solo or combined with purse or long nets, which means I can net up slightly less rigidly, and can use long nets more in the ferreting field. This is because I know with confidence that if a rabbit does run in a different direction from where I have set the long nets, or if I have missed a hole when setting purse nets, the dog will quickly pick up the offending rabbit. I am quite honestly surprised that more ferreters do not use long nets, as I still find the large

percentage will swear by using only purse nets, even though they are spending half of their time in the field setting nets.

Ferreting aside, what other purpose could a purse net have? Well, first ask yourself how many times you have seen a rabbit hop into a small gate drain, or a hole with only an entrance and exit under an old log pile or similar. If you carry a couple of purse nets with you, you can simply set them over the holes and then use a stick or whatever is to hand to flush

A rabbit securely balled up in a hemp purse net made by the author; this net has a double-pegging system in operation.

The same net as on the opposite page: the rabbit has no chance of escape as both rings of the net have met securely.

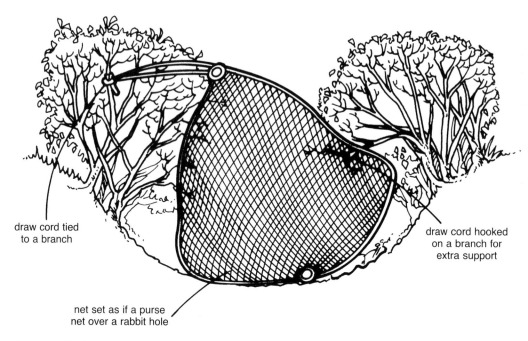

draw cord tied
to a branch

draw cord hooked
on a branch for
extra support

net set as if a purse
net over a rabbit hole

A hedge / ditch net set along the bottom of a ditch line.

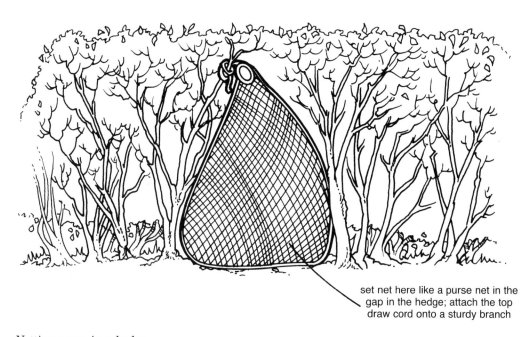

set net here like a purse net in the
gap in the hedge; attach the top
draw cord onto a sturdy branch

Netting a gap in a hedge.

the bunny out into the waiting net. I have also used purse nets to block gaps in hedges or runs in ditches when out shooting, and have accounted for a good many rabbits by always carrying a couple of trusty purse nets with me.

Hedge and Ditch Nets

Hedge and ditch nets are basically very large purse nets that can be tied to a branch in the hedge or pegged to a ditch to block a run or escape route. I make mine to a size of 5ft (1.5m) long by a mesh of $2^1/_8$in (5.4cm), but knit them twenty-two meshes wide as opposed to the fifteen on my purse nets. The only other difference to my purse nets is that I use larger rings and do not peg the bottoms. The weight of the large ring compensates for

the lack of the bottom peg, and stops the nets slipping too much.

Returning briefly to the purse net, I have also used purse nets during the summer to net up small burrows that I know the rabbits are feeding out from when I have not had a long net to hand. I have back-netted the quarry after I have flushed it from the area it is feeding in or inhabiting.

Gate Nets

Gate nets are another very overlooked tool, and can be used for a variety of purposes. As with all the nets mentioned, the usual mediums apply for materials, and as always they are generally made from nylon in 4oz or 6oz and in the standard 2in (5cm) mesh. Again, the same applies

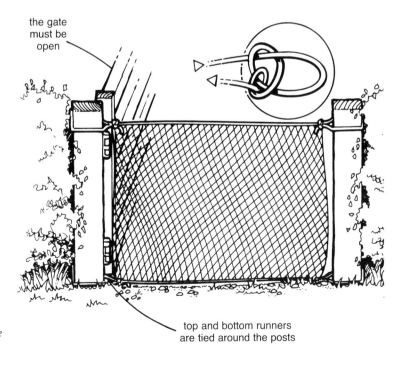

the gate
must be
open

top and bottom runners
are tied around the posts

An example of a set gate net.

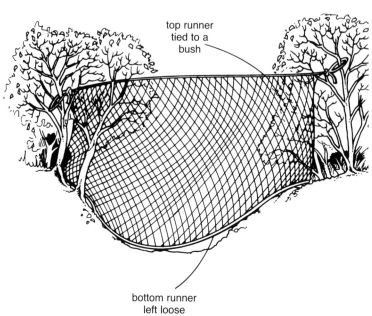

top runner
tied to a
bush

*A gate net being used as
a stop net across a ditch
line where a standard
ditch net would be too
small.*

bottom runner
left loose

to mesh sizes as it does for long nets, and I prefer to work gate nets with a $2\frac{1}{4}$in (5.6cm) to $2\frac{1}{2}$in (6.3cm) mesh size; the exception is a gate net being used for hares, when I would use a $2\frac{3}{4}$in (7cm) mesh; these will also hold rabbits if the net has enough slack. A gate net normally measures between 10ft and 20ft (3m and 7m), and as the name suggests it is used to block an open gateway so that any quarry flushed from the field becomes entangled.

The height varies, but it is generally about 5ft (1.5m). I use gate nets very regularly as stop nets for ferreting, especially in areas where a long net would be too long, such as in a small gap in a hedge. I also often run them across strategic gaps in rides when pushing through cover, with reasonable success. I would suggest that owning a couple of gate nets will prove well worthwhile, and as with purse nets,

carrying one rolled up in a pocket when out with the dog or rough shooting can often add a couple more head to the catch.

When used in their correct fashion of being set across a gateway, a gate net has no pegs to support it and is generally attached to the gate posts by cords that are attached to each corner of the net; these cords are tied to the gate's most usefully positioned branch. In some parts of the country the net will have a runner on the top and bottom just like a long net; in other areas runners are not used. I have used gate nets with and without runners, and find those with a top and bottom runner do seem to operate with more success than those without. When setting the net out of context on a ride or similar, the net can often be attached to a tree trunk or branch, but if it is being used as a stop net it will need to be supported on pegs just like a long net.

CHAPTER 9

NET-MAKING

Let us say that you have decided that you want to produce your own nets from scratch: so what are the advantages and disadvantages of doing so? The most obvious advantage is that if you make your own nets you can do so to the exact size and shape you want for use in the field; in most cases it is also cheaper to make your own than to buy. The big disadvantage is that net-making is extremely time-consuming, and you will need to decide how many hours you can afford to put into it; though of course you could always compromise and buy some nets, and then make just a few, as I must confess I have done occasionally!

Materials and Cost

No matter what sort of nets you intend to make, the materials that we have already mentioned are the ones that you are most likely to want to knit with. You can purchase nylon in 4oz (113g) and 6oz (170g) strengths, but it really does cut into your hands when knitting – in fact I would only ever use this to knit a long net. By far the easiest method with nylon nets in 4oz, 6oz and also 10z (284g) strength is to buy what is called sheet netting. This is a large length of prefabricated netting normally 150yd (137m) in length by a 2in (5cm) mesh that you can simply cut to the size you want and then use to construct gate, purse, hedge or long nets without too much hassle; to my mind this is a very easy way to get nets of a reasonable quality.

The Basic Equipment

The twines that are available for the person intending to make nets are hemp, spun nylon, nylon, cotton and jute/garden twine.

Hemp
A natural fibre that is very easy to knit, brown in colour, and generally in four or five ply. It is normally a rough texture, but a polished form can be purchased for a slightly higher price. The main drawback is that hemp rots if it is not dried out after use. A 0.5kg (1.2lb) ball costs around £8 to £10, and will make fifteen to twenty nets.

Spun nylon
A woollen form of nylon and is excellent for knitting with. It does not rot, and is also very easy to handle and comes in a variety of colours and thicknesses. I cannot find any drawbacks with this material, and it is my favourite for purse and gate nets. A 1kg (2.2lb) ball costs £18 to £20 and will make thirty to forty-five nets.

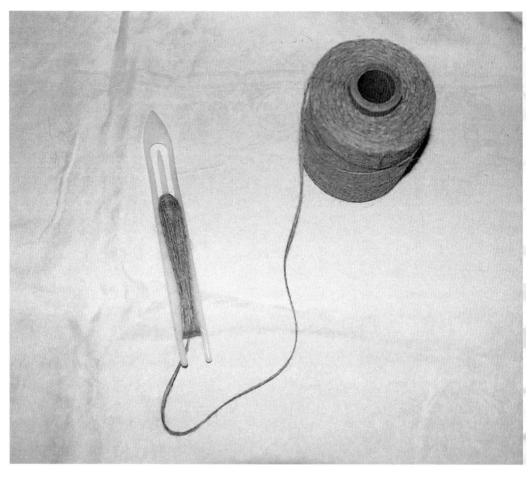

Spool of hemp twine.

Nylon
In twine form this can be purchased in 4oz, 6oz and 12oz (340g) strengths, 4oz being the weakest (40lb breaking strain) and 12oz the strongest. I never knit with 4oz or 6oz – unless I am really desperate – as it needs to be double knotted and cuts badly into your skin if you are making a lot of nets; 12oz is not as bad, although it does still take some handling to knit with. By far the easiest option is to buy nylon sheet netting, as mentioned above! Nylon costs around £5 to £8 a

0.5kg spool, depending on type; 4oz to 6oz makes forty-five to sixty nets, and 12oz eight to fourteen a spool.

Cotton
I have made nets from heavy-duty cotton, and by this I mean the type you use to tie up parcels. It is relatively cheap, and does make good nets that can be dyed to your choice of colour. However, it has no set breaking strain or strength, so if you do not use a good one of five to seven ply, it is likely to simply break on impact.

Cotton/string is an ideal choice for the beginner, because given its cost you can make good nets, but can afford to make mistakes at the same time. A 0.5kg spool costs £5 to £8 and will make twelve to twenty nets.

Jute/garden twine

Do not get this confused with hemp, because it is of much poorer quality, and is not designed for net-making as it has no set breaking strain. That said, I have obtained some very cheap jute that has made some excellent purse nets and has lasted for years; again, it is a good material for the beginner to use.

Where to Buy Twines

Most of the twines listed above can be sourced from larger field sports suppliers or specialist net suppliers that can be found advertising in the main field sports magazines such as *The Countryman's Weekly*. Twines such as jute and cotton are easier to obtain, and as mentioned are a lot cheaper, but they are of much poorer quality than hemp and spun nylon. Cotton twine and jute can be sourced from just about anywhere, from garden centres to hardware stores. The best bet is to keep your eyes open and to find the best quality products at the best prices.

Other Equipment

As well as twines, there are a few other things that you will need in order to make nets.

Rings

For both purse nets and long nets you will need the rings to attach your nets to at each end. Again, the best type is to be obtained from net-making suppliers, and is a steel ring that is plated to prevent rust. They are generally 1in (2.5cm) in diameter, and are welded shut to ensure they are totally solid; they are extremely cheap to buy at about 8p each, and are designed for net-making. Larger ones can be purchased, generally in $1^1/_2$in (3.8cm) or 2in (5cm) diameters. These are mainly suitable for larger nets such as fox nets or hedge nets, and are too heavy for standard rabbit nets.

An alternative to the above if you are really stuck is to use some curtain rings, which are, again, easy to obtain, and cheap, from most hardware stores. These rings are nowhere near as good as the steel ones, but I occasionally use them for nets if I am running low on kit.

Draw cord

This is a nylon twine normally $^1/_8$ to $^1/_4$in (2mm to 5mm) thick, and is ideal for the runners for nets as it slides so well against most materials. Again this can be purchased in spools, normally of about 200 to 300yd (183 to 274m), from net suppliers at a very reasonable cost. It is generally white, but can be obtained in different colours from time to time, depending on the supplier you use. It is also possible to buy this from hardware stores, but it costs a lot more and is generally bought by the yard or metre as opposed to buying it by the spool.

As already mentioned, I often use a thicker cord for my long-net draw cords. This is also nylon cord but is much heavier duty, and is something I have to shop around for; although I can buy it from hardware shops I have found the cheapest place to get it is from a chandler's shop, where it is again bought by the spool.

The peg

The final thing you will need for purse nets are the pegs that will hold the net in place. These are easily made from hazel, but again, can be bought from a variety of places. You can use plastic or metal tent pegs, or plastic garden netting pegs, all of which are easily purchased from a variety of stores if you choose not to cut your own. As well as using hazel pegs I also use any scraps of hardwood to cut pegs for purse nets; these make surprisingly fancy pegs, given my limited wood-working skills!

The final things you will need to make nets, apart from the all-important twines, are a good knife or a pair of scissors to cut your twine, a mesh-board, and a needle.

A mesh-board

This is probably the most important part of all of your kit, as it will determine the size of the meshes you are going to knit. A mesh-board can be made from just about any material and will be used to form every mesh on your net; the size of it will determine the mesh size, so if you want a 2in (5cm) mesh you will need a 2in mesh-board. I make my mesh-boards from mdf in a thickness of $^3/_8$in (1cm) or from plywood of $^3/_{16}$in (5mm) thick.

The important thing to remember is that the width of your mesh-board needs to be taken into account. By this I mean that if your mesh-board is $^3/_8$in (10mm) thick and you want a mesh-board of 2in, you will need to ensure that the $^3/_8$in width is taken into account so your board will actually be $^3/_8$in short of 2in.

In the table below, I have suggested the following sizes for meshes on nets; I have combined this by the size I would recommend making your nets to in width and length for the best results.

Mesh size	Type of net	Length	Width
1in	rat nets	$1^1/_2$–2ft	15 meshes
$1^1/_2$in	rat nets	2ft	13 meshes
2in	rabbit purse net	3–$4^1/_2$ft	15–18 meshes
2in	long net	50yd (100yd)	15–18 meshes
2in	long net	75yd (150yd)	15–18 meshes
2in	long net	100yd (200yd)	15–18 meshes
$2^1/_8$in	rabbit purse net	4–5ft	13–15 meshes
$2^1/_8$in	hedge/ditch net	5–$6^1/_2$ft	15–20 meshes
$2^1/_8$in	long nets	sizes as above	13–15 meshes
$2^1/_4$in	long nets	sizes as above	12–13 meshes
$2^1/_4$in	hedge/ditch net	5–$6^1/_2$ft	15–20 meshes
$2^3/_4$in	gate net hare	12–20ft	13–18 meshes
$2^3/_4$in	stop net hare/rabbit	12–20ft	13–18 meshes
3in	fox nets	5–$6^1/_2$ft	20–25 meshes

Needles
The final piece of all-important kit after your mesh-board is your needle to knit with, because without this you won't get very far! The net-maker's needle is generally now made from plastic, but traditionally it would be made from wood. Needles come in a variety of lengths and sizes, and the best advice I can give is to buy one that will fit through your rings, probably about 9in long and 1in in diameter.

I use this size, but also have a larger needle for long nets that holds more twine, so therefore don't have to do so many joins. Net needles are best purchased from specialist supply shops, but they can occasionally be bought from chandlers.

Making a Purse Net

So you have bought yourself some hemp

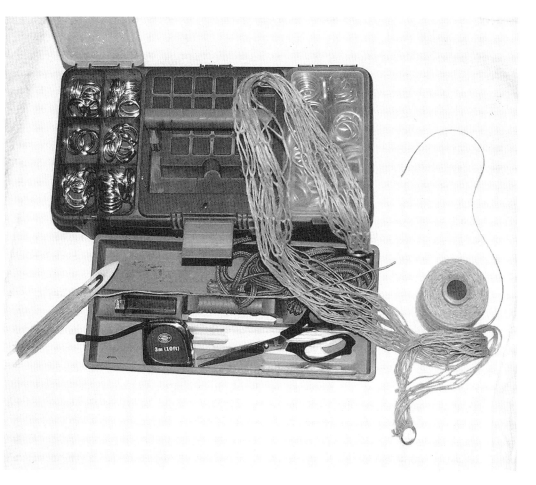

A box like this can be ideal for holding net-making equipment.

Essential net-making kit: scissors, mesh-board, twine and rings.

or spun nylon, and intend to make your first purse net. Nevertheless, however keen and well intentioned you are, the reality is that your first net is going to resemble a somewhat misshapen shopping bag – so don't set your expectations too high!

First you will need something to hold your net in place whilst you construct it. I attach a piece of draw cord/runner to a very strong radiator, and use this as my tether point to construct my net from; if you do not use a tether you will find it impossible to shape the meshes evenly as you work your way down the net.

The starting point with making a purse net is to attach your twine to the ring that will be your top end of the net. To do this you will need to load your twine on to the needle, and then once you have cut the twine loose from the spool, you can tie the loose end to the ring. There are only two knots that you really need in order to construct a net: the knot to attach the net to the end ring, and the one you will use on the meshes that you make.

The first knot used to secure the twine to the ring (if you are using nylon it is a good idea to heat-seal the knot to stop it slipping).

The knot you will use to attach your twine along the ring is difficult to describe, but I would say that the closest official knot is a clove hitch. You will find that by nature this knot slips, so I would suggest doubling it to ensure that it really binds tight; alternatively, after forming the clove hitch, you can form a sheet bend to secure the net firmly in place. You must ensure that your knots tied on to the ring are formed correctly, and that they are tight; these knots will be the founding point for the rest of your net, so need to be correctly tied.

After attaching the first knot to the ring it is time to get the mesh-board into use. Hold the board between your finger and thumb, and pull the twine behind it; then bring the twine and the needle over the front of it. Place the needle and twine through the ring, then form your knot on to the body of the ring and pull it tight. This will give you your first mesh, and the formation of your net.

An example of a clove hitch. This knot needs to be supported on both sides or it will slip, therefore a second knot to securely support it is advisable.

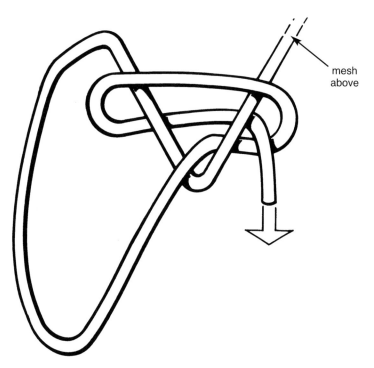

mesh above

The sheet bend is the most important knot in net-making.

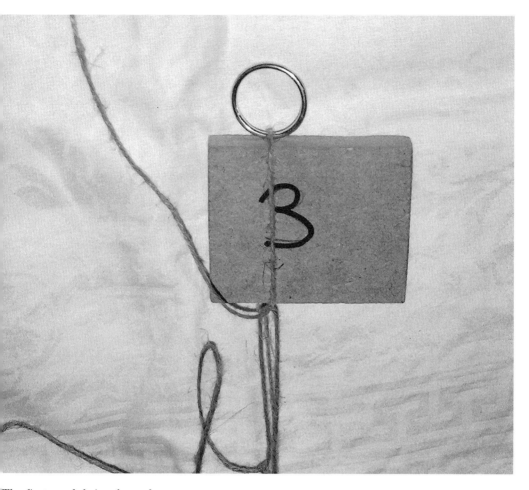

The first mesh being formed.

Repeat this process until you have put the full number of meshes on to the ring to make the width of the net that you require. Once you have done this you will be ready to construct your second row of the net.

To do this, remove your mesh-board and place it below the last mesh that you have constructed on the ring. Again, hold the bottom of the mesh with your thumb and finger against the top of the board; then, as when you started, pull the twine behind it, and then over the front of it and through the mesh that you are holding, in the same manner as when attaching the first row to the ring.

The difference now is in the type of knot, because you will need to use a sheet bend to construct the meshes on this row, and all the rows down the net. A sheet bend is an easy knot: the important bit is to ensure that you pull the knot tight on to the bottom of the mesh you are attaching it to, because if you get this part

A sheet bend being formed before being pulled tight.

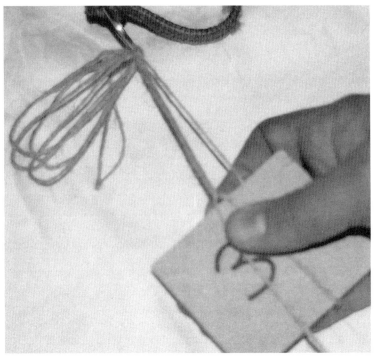

Holding the twine to the mesh board while forming a mesh.

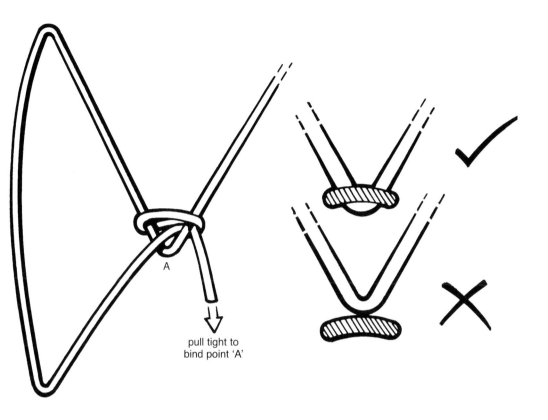

pull tight to
bind point 'A'

The sheet bend must be secured and pulled tight to the bottom of the mesh it is being formed to.

wrong the mesh you are forming will not hold tight and will slip, making the meshes useless.

Now repeat this process along the row of meshes until you have constructed the entire length of the net and are in a position to attach it to the second end ring that will complete your net. When this point comes, all you have to do is repeat your first steps but in reverse until you have attached the final row of meshes to the ring and can cut the twine from the ring. This done, you will have completed your first purse net minus the drawer cord.

Knitting with Nylon

When you knit using nylon you need to bear in mind that using a single sheet bend is not enough. The problem with nylon is its texture, as it is a very smooth-running twine and will easily slip if just a single sheet bend is used. You therefore need to double your knots when using nylon, to stop the knots slipping. This is a very straightforward process of simply repeating the process on each mesh; thus the first knot tied on to each mesh will support the mesh you have created, and

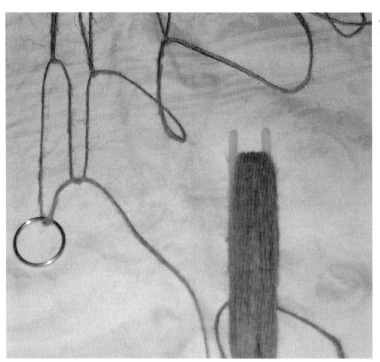

Attaching the last row of meshes to the end ring.

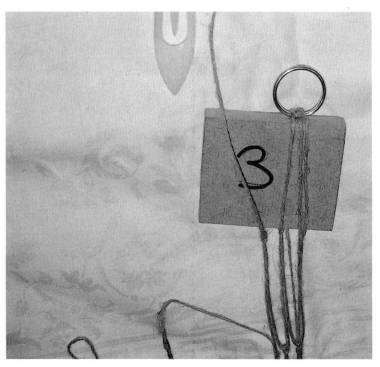

Sowing meshes onto the end ring and securing them to the end ring with a double knot.

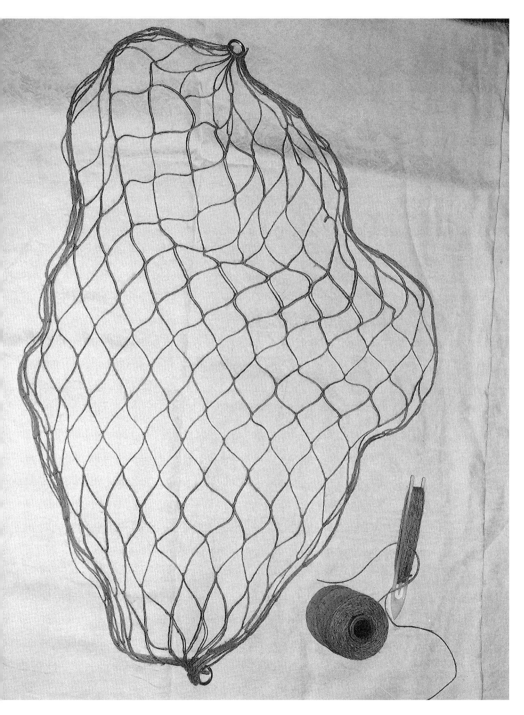

A completed net.

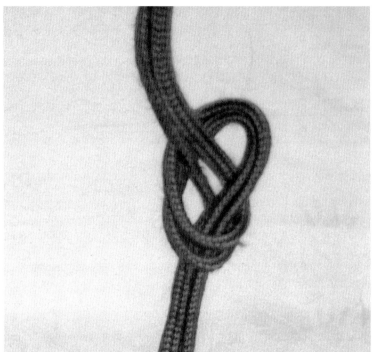

The knot used to join lengths of twine together, again, if this is nylon twine it is advisable to heat-seal the knot.

A net being formed with extra meshes being added in to each row.

he second knot will act as a support to stop the first knot slipping.

There is some variation as to how people do this. Some form the sheet bend twice, by which I mean that instead of passing the twine through the mesh once, they do it two times, and then pull the whole knot tight. My own preference is to form one knot and then another directly afterwards, as I find this is much easier than trying to make a double-looped knot.

Sheet Netting and Nylon

We have already discussed sheet netting and the advantages of using it as opposed to actually knitting in nylon due to its rather nasty habit of cutting into your fingers and hands – a fact I can confirm as I am just completing a batch of 100 12oz nylon nets for a friend, and my hands as a result are cut to ribbons.

Sheet netting can be a godsend should you insist for some strange reason in only using nylon nets. It is simplicity itself to make nets from this product. All you have to do is cut a length of the sheet to the length you want your purse net to be, and then simply attach your end rings to the sheet you have cut. To do this you just load a needle and attach the loose piece of twine from it to the first mesh you are going to attach to the first end ring. You then knit the row of meshes to the ring so they are secured, and do the same for the second end ring; you will then have a nylon purse net ready for use, except for attaching the draw cord.

Traditional Nets and Bourse Nets

The method described so far is the basic way of making a good, usable purse net;

however, as you may have discovered already if you are sewing a large amount of meshes on to a ring, it can become a bit of a squeeze and as a result can put the shape of your net slightly out. The answer to this is to taper your net from the ring and to expand it as you reach the centre of your net, then to taper it back in again as you go towards the end ring of your net. This is a process that seems off-putting to start with, but is really easy once you get the hang of it.

Let's say that you want to make a net that will become eighteen meshes wide at its centre, but you don't want to sew eighteen meshes on to the ring. Start as with a normal net, but sew ten meshes on to the ring, then do the same on to the second row. When you come to the third row you will need to add a mesh in. To do this, sew the first two or three meshes on as normal, then before you sew the fourth or fifth mesh, add a mesh in by forming it around the mesh-board and then knotting it in place above the last knot you formed on your second or third mesh.

You will have what looks like half a mesh added to the row, and when you start your next row you can simply form a mesh around it, thus making an extra mesh. It is then a case of repeating this process on every row or couple of rows until you reach the size you require for the centre of the net. Once you have reached the maximum mesh width you want, it is best to knit at least five rows at this width to ensure that the centre of your net is a good size to operate and to hold a bolting rabbit.

When you have done this and are starting to work your way towards completing your net, you can easily taper the net in by pulling two meshes together as you work downwards, and tying your knot

A part-made net showing the meshes starting to form.

around the two meshes to reduce the row by a mesh at a time.

Be careful not to go too quickly at this stage, as you may find that you have knitted your meshes to a smaller width than you intended by tying too many meshes together. The net that I make and use as standard in the field, and that I am 100 per cent satisfied with, is tapered, starting off as nine meshes on the ring, then increasing by one mesh every two lines until it reaches a width of twenty meshes in the centre. I then sew four rows of twenty meshes in place, before working my way downwards taking in one mesh every two rows until I reach the nine meshes that I started with. This gives me a net that measures about 4ft 6in in length, and is wide enough at its centre to

easily hold a rabbit in place once it has bolted.

This is my perfect type of net that I am more than happy to use in the field. Most important is to ensure that the draw cord is long enough to support the net, and to allow the meshes to slip easily along the cord when set. I hate nets with tiny draw cords, and always add a long cord to my purse nets, with plenty of play in it so that I can peg my nets with ease or remove the peg and tie the cord to a fence or branch if needs be. Furthermore I seldom use nets with only one peg attached, because when a standard net is set and pegged in the normal way, it is very easy for the net to slip when a rabbit hits it, and for the rabbit to bounce its way to freedom. Over the years I have lost countless numbers of rabbits because of this, and have found that the solution is to peg the nets at both ends.

I have a long draw cord on the top of my net, and peg this in the normal manner; I also have a very short length of cord on the bottom of my net, and peg this into the bottom, or the mouth of the rabbit hole. When the net is set like this, and if it opens up correctly over the hole when a rabbit hits the net and becomes balled up, the net pulls against itself and the rabbit is unable to break free. This may sound strange but I have found it works wonders, and it really has saved me countless numbers of rabbits.

One final difference I make to my own nets compared to most normal nets is that from time to time I will double-strand my meshes. By 'double stranding' I mean that each mesh consists of two lines of twine, as opposed to one. To do this I simply load my needle with two twines at the same time, with the result that you end up with a net that effectively can be made with slightly larger meshes, as the double-twined mesh seems to form an extra loop. I do not double-twine all of my nets but have made a few like this as I find they are particularly useful on burrows were the holes are really large. As I net on a lot of sandy ground this is often the case, and these double-twined nets seem to cover the holes much better than a single-stranded net.

Rat and Fox Nets

Although we are primarily dealing with rabbit nets, I feel that the role of rat and fox nets in the field, and the way they are formed, is worthy of mention. Firstly a fox net is basically a large purse net with larger meshes, and is formed in exactly

the same way; it has the same use as a rabbit purse, but is used on foxes that are being flushed with terriers.

Ferrets can be worked to rats as well as to rabbits, and you can purse-net rats as well as you can rabbits, again as with a fox net. Purse nets for rats are made in a smaller mesh size than a rabbit net, and of course in a smaller length. I have also in the past made stop nets for rats in a small mesh size – though I must admit this was a long and tedious task due to the small meshes, and it is not one I want to repeat! A basket-type net can also be made for rats, though I have to confess that I have never tried to make one of these, nor have I seen one made; I therefore feel it would not be right for me to describe the process, as I would not be doing so from experience. As far as I am concerned, purse-netting rats is always a last resort: I much prefer to shoot them or to use dogs to deal with this quarry, as I am petrified of being bitten whilst trying to despatch one in a net!

Making Long Nets

I do not want to go into this subject too exhaustively, but will simply describe the way in which I was taught to make long nets, and still do today. There are variations on this, but I will stay with what I know because I find it is the easiest method to make a net. I simply start my long net in the same way that I would a purse net – but be aware that tapering is not an option, so you will need to sew the correct meshes on to the ring right from the start.

I normally knit my long nets to a $2^{1}/_{4}$in or $2^{1}/_{8}$in mesh size by thirteen meshes in width, and simply sew the start of my net

Sheet netting and net-making kit, including a spun nylon long net under construction.

on to a large end ring. I then knit the net just as I would a purse net, but of course the more of the net you knit, the less there will be of the cord you are using to pull your net tight, and it will eventually run out. You will therefore find that you will need to thread your support cord through the meshes the more you knit –

remember you will be knitting perhaps a hundred yards or more of netting!

Once you have completed your net you do not need to add an end ring and can cut the ring off from where you started. The final step is to add your runners, which is the hardest part of all. First you need to make sure they are both cut to the correct length, because if they are even a yard out this will make the net uneven on the top and bottom. To attach your runners takes time, and by far the easiest way I have found it is to hook the net up in 10yd (9m) lengths, and then thread one of the runners through until it is completely attached and secured in place by knotting at each end.

The second runner can then be added in the same manner, and the final task is now to run the net out fully, and to spread the slack out so that it is reasonably even. At this point I then tie in the net to the runners at roughly the same distance as I will set my pegs.

To make a long net in this manner if you are prepared to knit, say, two hours a day, will probably take you about six to seven weeks to knit 100yd (91m) for a 50yd (46m) net. You may therefore opt for the cheating method, namely our old friend sheet netting. As you can imagine, sheet netting cuts out the knitting part, and you simply need to add your runners, which can be a much quicker alternative if you simply cannot find a ready-made long net that suits your needs. You will also have to consider the fact that if you want a net of, say, 100yd with a 100yd of slack, you will have to at some point join lots of sheet net together, as I tend to find that sheet netting is only really available in 150yd (136m) lengths. Again this is a simple task of matching up the last row from each sheet, and with your netting needle, tying the row together with a double-sheet bend on each joining mesh.

The method described for making long nets can also be used to produce gate nets or smaller stop nets, which will, of course, take a lot less time to construct.

Net-Making for Profit

You should now know enough of the basics to make your own purse nets, and possibly even feel sufficiently confident to attempt to make a long net or gate net. Be warned, however, that if you now have thoughts of producing mass amounts of nets for sale, this is probably not a good idea. Making purse nets for personal use is most certainly a cheap and rewarding process, but trying to make purse nets for sale is the exact opposite.

To buy a good quality purse net will cost no more than a top price of £3.50; to make a net for yourself to an equal, if not superior standard, will cost you about £1.50 to £2 net in hemp or spun nylon. The problem comes in the time it takes to make one, because to produce a good net, even with an excellent net-maker, will probably take at least an hour. With this in mind it is easy to see that if you took the minimum wage and added your material costs to a net to make a profit, you would need to sell your nets for about £7.50 each, which is a somewhat high cost to try to meet. Long nets are even worse, and I can assure you that making a long net for profit is even more difficult. This is something I learned with experience, and it is an experience I do not intend to repeat. Take my advice and make nets as a hobby or for your own use, but *not for profit*, as I guarantee you will lose out in the long run!

CHAPTER 10

STORIES FROM THE FIELD

So far we have looked at using long nets and other nets in the field, and have also discussed net-making in enough detail for you to be able to produce, I would hope, some home-made nets for your own use. So now I thought might be a good time to relate some of my own experiences in the field, to show how well, or badly, things can go! Firstly, as already mentioned, I do not claim to be an expert on netting, or indeed ferreting, but have written this simply as someone who enjoys this activity, and wishes to pass on what he knows about it to others, in order to ensure its future in a time when entertainments such as computer games and television are much more popular than the idea of going out on a cold wet night to bag a few rabbits.

Tailing Your Nets

A good starting point might be to describe how I discovered that rabbits are not quite as silly as people think. I had been out on a couple of occasions to a large field that was full of rabbits, and had bagged a few with my .22 rifle; but because I am a considerably poor shot I decided it might be a better idea to

venture forth with a long net in a bid to get a reasonable catch. This was during the summer months, when the field was laid up to grass for hay.

I knew that by dawn the rabbits were always feeding well into the field, and that it would be an easy matter to set a net between them and their burrows because the grass was so long, and also because a useful slope would help conceal it; so I set forth at dawn with the dog and a couple of nets, on a day when there was going to be a breeze in my favour and a little early morning mist to cover any of our movement. Everything went as planned, and I had the nets set in about five minutes, and then made my way to the other side of the field to run the catch home.

I could see several heads and ears poking up and sniffing around in the grass, and began to run the dog through the cover with the intention of then quickly removing my large haul and heading for home. But as I neared the net I could clearly see that there was no movement in it, but could not work out why it was. Then I noticed a brace of rabbits hop out slowly towards the net, in no rush whatsoever. This is often one of the problems of netting at dawn rather than at night, as he rabbits do not hit the nets with such speed as when they are flushed after dark.

The next thing I saw was that the rabbits stopped dead at the net, then ran its full length and casually passed behind it and to safety. I watched another ten or so do this before I finally got close enough with the dog to speed the last few up and force them into the net. The problem was that I had not tailed the net, which is why the rabbits managed to run its length and get behind it without any problem or alarm. If, however, the net had been tailed (brought round into the field almost at right angles), when they reached the end of its length they would still have hit netting, and would either have been caught, or been so flustered that they would've turned back towards the dog or the net and been easily caught. This is why you should always tail your nets!

Despatching Your Rabbit

My second story relates to the despatching of rabbits, often a difficult first-time task for the novice. There are three main ways to kill a rabbit, and it is your responsibility to ensure that you respect your quarry and kill it quickly so that it doesn't suffer. I now use the method known as 'chinning'; in this, you hold the rabbit by the back legs, and place your middle and index finger on either side of its head, with your finger running from behind the ears and along the bottom of the jaw/chin; then quickly pull your hand and the rabbit's head down, and then sharply upwards to break its neck. This will despatch it quickly and with no suffering, as the whole operation takes about a second at most.

The other two methods are just as quick: one involves using a priest to issue a quick, sharp blow to the back of the rabbit's head; the other involves the same procedure but using the back of your hand (known as the 'rabbit chop'). However, be sure you know how to carry out this 'chop' effectively: on one of my first days ferreting I decided to go for the chop that I had read about in a book, and duly went on to hit half-a-dozen rabbits on the back of the neck using this method. I then placed the rabbits, as I dealt with them, into a hessian sack to keep them cool, and went back to the ferreting.

All was going well until I noticed the sack had moved about ten yards, which seriously puzzled me. I then also noticed that it seemed rather flat, and on peering in was startled by a rabbit exiting at high speed. It turned out that I hadn't got the procedure of the chop quite right, and although I had managed to stun the rabbits slightly, had certainly not despatched them, and they had come round and escaped to freedom!

I would therefore always advise that you know how to despatch your quarry properly before you attempt to do it, obviously to prevent it escaping, but more importantly, to ensure that you give it the respect it deserves by despatching it as quickly and as painlessly as possible.

Follow Your Instincts

There are, of course, times when everything goes as planned, and I recall a most successful netting trip one cold December night. I was about to leave home to go and put my horse into her stable at about

7pm, when I realized that the wind was good for a netting trip – a stiff breeze, but not too strong – so I decided to take a couple of nets with me, and try the small field next to the field my horse was in. We had ferreted the hedge bordering this field a couple of weeks previously, but had not had great success as the warren in the hedge was a good three hundred holes, and stretched for at least 200yd; it was also in sand and therefore very deep, making ferreting hard work rather than fun.

I knew the weather was right and I was hopeful the rabbits would be out feeding, as I normally visited the area at about 5pm to check the horse, and the landowner walked his dog at about 10pm. Therefore the rabbits would go out to feed between 6pm and 10pm, when they knew they would not be disturbed. These rabbits tended never to feed out late at night, because they would wait to come out and feed again at dawn; so everything looked promising, as I would be at the ground for about 7.30pm.

On my arrival the wind had picked up slightly but was still not too strong, and it was blowing in the right direction for me to creep round the edge of the top field and pass unnoticed into the bottom field a hundred yards further down. I reached my destination and pulled the first 75yd (68m) net from my pocket. The anchor pin was pushed into the hard winter ground, and I then ran the net down the length of the hedge until I felt it pull tight; I then secured the second anchor pin.

The second net – this time a 100yd net – was then pulled out, and the anchor pin pushed through the last few yards of the first net; I then ran this net to its full length, and tailed it. This took all of two

minutes, and it took just another minute to walk the length of both nets and put the pegs in place, since the field was really smooth and free of any twigs or debris.

I then made my way as silently as could up to the top field, retracing my original steps. I had not seen any movement in the field but the moon wasn't even visible and I could barely see my own hand, let alone a yard into the field. After what seemed an eternity – but was in fact no time at all – I had approached the far side of the field and was in a position to drive the rabbits home. This field is not large and the rabbits have been dogged quite hard, so all I had to do was switch on a high-powered lamp and shine it across the field, as I knew this would send any rabbits straight for home. don't usually use a lamp for netting, but had it with me for checking the horse so thought I would use it to my advantage.

The beam shone out brightly into the crisp, still air and, as I had hoped, picked up several sets of red eyes shining brightly from about two hubdred yards out in the field. The rabbits were aware of my presence, and were squatting tightly around clumps of grass that were moulded into a rough green pattern across the field. I stepped forwards, still shining the lamp, and after taking a few steps the first coney sprang for home and dashed across the field. I lost sight of it after a few yards, as a hazy winter mist was setting in.

I zigzagged the short distance back to the net, and on reaching the centre could feel it jumping, which indicated a good catch. On walking the full length I removed thirteen healthy rabbits, and lost probably another five from a section of net where I had not set enough slack

The whole interlude had taken about half an hour, and I was more than happy with the return.

This is just one example of when everything goes right, and shows that in many cases you cannot pre-plan a netting trip, and that it is just a case of watching the weather and going with your instincts.

Night-Time Encounters

I remember one occasion that gave me much more than I bargained for. It happened long before I was much good at netting, and just showed that there is often a lot more about at night than you expect. I had asked my then girlfriend (now my wife) if she would like to go for a moonlit stroll on the downs close to home, and thinking that I was being romantic, she duly accepted. I then ruined the moment by loading a long net and pegs on to the back of my motorbike, explaining that she could assist me with some netting that I was keen to do, in response to a request from a farmer.

For some reason she agreed, and we were soon walking up the steep hillside towards a small covert full of rabbit burrows. The rabbits here feed right out on the hillside, and it was easy to set nets without them knowing because they were feeding over a ridge and wouldn't have had any idea that we were there.

I started setting the net, and then got a strange feeling – in fact a feeling I often get, in common with a lot of people who are in a sense hunters, a sort of sixth sense, which made me feel sure that someone or something else was present in my surroundings. I grabbed a light that my partner had brought, and shone it to my left where I felt sure I would pick up a badger or fox watching us.

As the light shone out I picked up a set of big green eyes about thirty yards away from me, and there, sitting flat on the ground, was a large black cat, like a panther. It looked at me, and I stood terrified, trying to think what to do next. The cat then stood up, and thankfully appeared to be more scared of me than I was of it; it moved off away from me, stopping about a hundred yards later to look back.

Netting was now the last thing on my mind; I quickly picked up my kit and, with my girlfriend in tow – who was still not too sure what we had seen – headed back to my bike at top speed. I am convinced that what I saw was a member of the big cat family, and since that occasion twelve years ago I have a few times again seen what I believe to be a big cat, though never so close up.

I have also had encounters with other people at night, and this can be just as unnerving. I once set up a large set of about 300yd (240m) of netting, and was just about to run any rabbits up the field when I felt a sharp jerk on the net. I made my way along it expecting to find a deer or a fox balled up – and found a lurcher, well and truly caught.

From the darkness three figures appeared and claimed the dog – and this situation presented me with a problem because they were poaching, and were not too happy that I had disturbed their illegal nocturnal activity. I in turn was not overly happy that they had ruined my set, but my main concern was the dog, as I did not want it to be injured in the net, but nor did I want it to ruin the said net – and so we agreed to work together to release it.

This took a good hour, but eventually it was freed, and with a successful outcome, since neither dog nor net were injured. Moreover in the space of this hour we lost all animosity towards each other due to our mutual interest in field sports, and agreed to put the incident down to experience, and to say no more about it. I did, however, make it clear that if I caught them on the ground again I would not let it pass and would have to take action. But they never did work it again, and set to poaching elsewhere. I must add that these characters were *not* what I would call major poachers out for profit, but rather pothunters who couldn't be bothered to get any permission, a state of affairs that I find very annoying, given the work I put into keeping my ground.

On a more amusing note I once set some long nets along a large field at dusk during the summer months. There were rabbits here in huge abundance, and as they had not been touched for years, they were proving easy to catch. I would almost reverse the process, and would set my nets along the hedge line at dusk, then disappear for an hour or so; on my return I would always find a dozen or so rabbits caught up as they ventured out to feed. This may sound a strange idea, but it worked on several occasions on the ground in question.

On this occasion I had pulled up to collect the nets, and on shining a light down the length of the net picked up some eyes half way down. Again at first I thought it was a fox, but then I noticed a second set of eyes about six foot up. I approached the eyes armed with a large stick, and found a Labrador dog and its owner trying to remove a very tangled rabbit from the net. The man explained that his dog had shot off from the footpath – a fair distance away – on a scent, and had failed to return, so he had gone to look for it and had found it here, with the rabbit in the net.

I duly removed the rabbit, and as no harm had been done was not bothered by the incident. The man asked if he could possibly take the rabbit for the dog, and as I had a freezer full of them already, I had no objections. But as he walked away I thought it strange that only one rabbit had been caught; and then I noticed that the man's coat was bulging somewhat – so I caught up to him, and completely by accident knocked into him, causing his coat to open.

A further ten rabbits fell from his coat, and it turned out that he had in fact removed these from the net. He explained that he thought he had just got lucky, and didn't know that the net had been set to catch rabbits, but had thought it was a fence of some sort, and was too embarrassed to say anything when I had appeared. As he was local and no real harm had been done I was happy for him to keep the rabbits, but politely asked him to leave them in the future. That was six years ago, and he still regularly walks in the area, but these days leaves my nets alone.

Conclusion

To conclude, I would say enjoy your pastime, but also be sure you remember why you are taking your quarry, and give it the respect it deserves. Remember to use the weather and the countryside to your advantage, and never underestimate the benefits of reconnaissance and fieldcraft, as this is the only way you will truly manage to get good results. Thus there is no point netting at night on ground where the rabbits always feed during the late afternoon or at dusk, or during the day when you know they feed between midnight and dawn or from dusk until 1am. And you will only know these things if you take the time to look around your ground, and learn how the quarry behaves. Take note of the runs and which way they go. Are there any passing points in hedges where it could pay to lay a hedge net or stop net? Are there a lot of runs in the morning dew going through a gateway, which could mean that if you went up an hour earlier and set a gate net you could end up with a brace of rabbits?

All these factors will help you improve your skills and your catches by helping you to be in the right place at the right time. This, combined with respecting the wishes of the landowner and acting in a responsible manner, will see you in sport for many years, and if you have a good reputation you will no doubt find that even more opportunities come your way.

These days most activities involving the control of live animals are under great threat, as many people who do not live and work in the country do not understand the need to control vermin. It is therefore most important that we do everything to promote and explain our activity to those who do not understand it, and that we conduct ourselves correctly in the field. For myself, I derive a measure of satisfaction from the fact that I am able to reduce a pest species in a professional manner, and can pass on my catch so that it does not go to waste; after all, what is more organic than a fresh-netted wild rabbit?

It is ensuring that the method of control is professionally and efficiently executed that gives me pleasure and enjoyment, and for this reason I intend to take part in field sports for the rest of my life; as for many country people, it is more than a pastime, it is a way of life. All I can say is, enjoy your sport, keep your nets dry and in good repair – and never give up.

CHAPTER 11

TRAPPING AND SNARING

Before I depart these pages and plan my next trip into the field I would like to pass comment on two subjects that may well help you to add to your catches, and also offer assistance to the reader who is still not convinced that long netting or netting in general on its own is for him or her.

The use of traps can be an easy and effective way of catching a few rabbits in areas where netting is simply not practical; in my experience this tends to be on burrows that are too large to ferret, or areas where the fields are too small to practically long net. Furthermore you are limited as to how often you can long net a field before you exhaust it, so trapping can be a good way of catching rabbits in between netting trips.

If you are going to do any trapping the first thing you will need to consider is the time involved, because you must ensure without exception that your traps are checked at least every twenty-four hours, and realistically I would suggest that any traps need to be checked at least once every twelve hours; the easiest way is to check them at dusk and dawn. As with netting, another important thing to consider regarding trapping is whether you can run traps without the risk of having them removed or damaged. There are

therefore two things to consider before doing any trapping: firstly, whether it is safe to use traps in an area where stock is grazing, or near buildings where there could be other animals such as the farmer's cat that could become trapped or stock such as cattle that could damage and destroy your traps. Secondly, is it going to be safe for you to use traps on your ground if you have footpaths running everywhere?

I never trap near public rights of access because firstly, a lot of people do not understand why someone wants to trap, and will not hesitate to destroy, damage or in some cases steal your traps. Also people who walk their dog on footpaths will sometimes let it run off the lead, and wouldn't be too happy if it sticks its nose down a hole and gets it stuck in a tunnel trap, or its foot caught in a snare set in an adjoining field. And although it should not have been in the field in the first place, it's no good arguing because this will not promote your activity.

In summary, if you are going to use traps, don't set them in areas where the public will easily see them, or where they could cause damage or injury to people or livestock. Make sure you have the time to check them at least twice daily; and always make sure the landowner knows where your traps are, and what you are planning to catch.

Snares for Rabbits

Let us first look at snares for rabbits. Snaring is possibly one of the most misunderstood ways of taking rabbits, considered by many to be extremely cruel when in fact if done properly – and I must emphasize 'properly' – it is a remarkably effective means of controlling rabbit numbers.

I have been running snares for the past seventeen years and, as with netting, have learned by my mistakes along the way. The snares I currently use are hand made, although snares can be purchased easily for about 20p to 30p each from a variety of places, from agricultural suppliers to gun shops. I make mine from brass picture wire that I purchase for the sum of 70p per 3m (10ft) from a high street chain; I then cut this to the size I require, and attach my eyelets to each wire. The 3m gives me about fifteen wires, and the eyelets cost me about £1 for 100, so very little cost is involved.

Your snares must be free-running, as snares that are stopped are illegal. By 'stopped' this means that a snare that is set must not have anything deliberately fitted on to it to stop it opening when it has been sprung, thereby preventing any caught animal from possibly releasing itself from the snare's noose.

A snare consists of three other components besides the noose: a support cord, a peg and a tealer. Firstly, the support cord runs from the noose to the peg that will hold the snare tightly in place when it is set, and must be very strong; the most common materials to use are spun nylon or baler twine, both of which seem to be fairly indestructible. The peg must therefore also be strong and true to form, and not surprisingly I make my own.

I use two materials for my pegs: hazel and elder. Hazel pegs I cut to a diameter of about $1\frac{1}{2}$in (38mm), with a point on one end, and a hole drilled out to hold the support cord. I prefer to use elder that I cut and dry; it is much lighter to carry than hazel, and seems to last a lot longer. Your pegs will rot in time and will need replacing, so it always pays to cut a few spare.

The final component is the tealer, a thin support stake used to hold the actual noose in place. A variety of different types are in use; my own chosen method, and one that I designed myself, is to use the thin, indoor type of plant support stakes. I attach brown rawlplugs on the top of these to sit my noose in, and they seem to work really well.

Snares need to be set on the rabbits' runs in order to work effectively, so firstly you need to make sure that you can identify a rabbit run – which is fairly easy to do. On a rabbit run you will notice a series of flat areas where the rabbit stops, and in between a series of longer tufts of grass that it jumps. For a wire to work effectively it needs to be set on the middle of the seat, so that as the rabbit jumps it heads straight into the noose. It is crucial that the rabbit is caught correctly to ensure that it does not suffer.

Some runs are so well used that there are no jumps visible, and these are even easier to wire, as you can set them just about anywhere. These runs are the sort that you often see leading from a field that has just been sown, and can produce some good catches. I have set some of these runs with two or three wires spread along the run at intervals of 20 or 30yd (18 or 27m), and have caught in every wire the following morning.

It is also possible to catch rabbits in gaps in hedges that lead out to runs, or in ditch lines; but if I have the choice I always prefer to set on runs. With gaps in hedges the best plan is to get rid of the peg and tealer, and to attach the wire via its cord to the hedge or fence above the gap. The wire should cover the whole of the gap, because when a rabbit is on a run it will be moving relatively quickly, but when coming out of a hedge it will be moving at a slower pace and will first poke its head out carefully. If your wire is too small it will sense it and move away from it, and then try to find another place to come through. But if your wire is set large the rabbit will poke its head through and then continue moving, and

as it goes forwards it will pull the noose and catch itself with ease. Setting wires in hedges may sound easy, but it takes a lot of time and patience to get it just right, and in my opinion it is a lot easier just to stay with snaring runs.

There is no point in setting ten wires when you have twenty runs, and to get good results you will need to set your wires on as many runs as you can. Remember that if you have twenty runs going into a field this does not mean you will have twenty rabbits to catch: in actual fact I would say that to twenty runs you will in most cases get a return of about five rabbits.

To work effectively I only snare areas where I know there is a real problem with rabbits, and where my time in setting my wires will not be wasted (I tend to run a hundred to three hundred wires at a

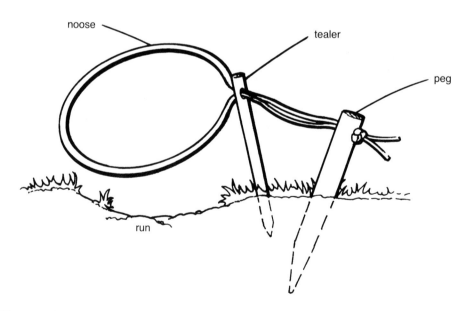

Front profile of a set snare.

Side profile of a set snare.

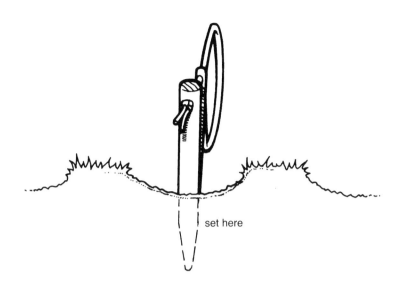

set here

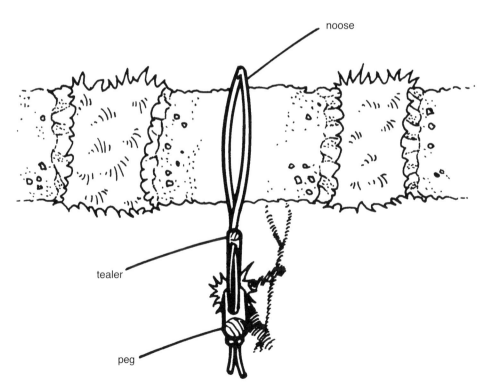

noose

tealer

peg

Overview of a set snare.

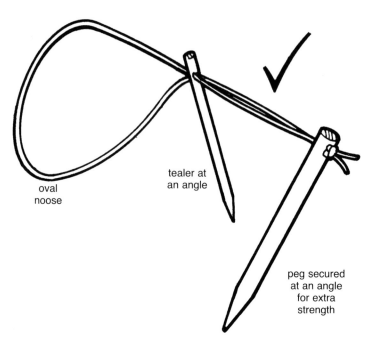

oval
noose

tealer at
an angle

peg secured
at an angle
for extra
strength

A set snare: note how the peg is set at an angle to stop it being pulled loose, and how the noose is more oval in shape than round.

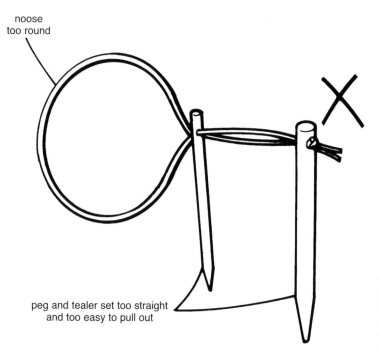

noose
too round

peg and tealer set too straight
and too easy to pull out

A snare set incorrectly, as the peg is not at an angle and will easily pull loose, and the noose is round in shape when it is best set oval.

A rabbit run clearly visible on some grass; always ensure if snaring that you can tell a rabbit run from other animals' runs.

time). I work by setting my wires at dawn when the runs are clearly visible in the morning frost or dew; I then leave them set for three nights, and pick them up at dawn after my final night set. I find that on the first night's set I get a minimal catch because no matter how carefully I have set my wires, there will always be some of my scent on them. The second night yields the best catch, and the final night picks up any stragglers. During the daytime you will also pick up a few, especially in areas when the rabbits feed out in the afternoon.

When you set your wires you will need a good hammer to knock your pegs in, and, most importantly, you will need to ensure they are set at the right height to catch your quarry correctly. As already mentioned, you need to catch your rabbit by the head just behind the ears, because if you do this, one of two things will happen: a clever rabbit will stop fighting against the wire and will sit still and tight, and when you check your wires you can then despatch it. Or it will struggle and pull against the wire, and basically will strangle itself – and cruel as it sounds, this will kill it in a very short space of time.

Your wire needs to be set so that the bottom of the wire will catch the bottom of the rabbit's chin, and the top will slide over its ears; I find that, rather than a round-shaped noose, a pear-shaped one works the best. If you are using new wires they will be very shiny, so before using them it is a good idea to hang them outside for a few days to take off the shine and to allow the very human smell they will carry to dissipate.

The height you will need to set the wire to catch the rabbit's chin will vary according to the type of ground you are going to work, but as a rule on a standard grass field you will need to set it about 5in (13cm) from the ground. On rougher ground or plough I find a little more height is needed, so I normally set my wires to a height of about 7in (18cm). If you set your wire too low or high the rabbits will just push it over and it will be useless. If the noose is set round and is too big you risk the rabbit being caught by the stomach or legs, which you don't want as this will cause distress and suffering to your quarry, which should be avoided at all costs.

When you set your wires you must be absolutely sure that you know where they are, so you can be sure that you don't leave any behind when you come to pick them up. There are various ways you can do this. My chosen method is to mark the first wire I set with a dot of white paint on the tealer and peg; I then set eight wires between this and the tenth, which I mark in the same way. One problem you will have is that any rabbits caught overnight, or even in the day, run the risk of being removed by predators – mainly foxes – before you get to them.

I have heard many ideas concerning how you can deter predators, especially foxes, from stealing your catch. The most well-known deterrent seems to be to attach a small bell to your wire, so that should a fox grab a caught rabbit the bell will tinkle and disturb the fox. I have tried this, and to be honest found that foxes would get used to the bells and would then still remove caught rabbits. To my mind there is no way that you can really stop foxes taking your catch. My best advice if you are working an area where foxes are known to prevail is to check your wires an hour or so after dark and just slightly before dawn. These seem to be the times when foxes tend to really hammer wires, and when you are most likely to catch them at it, or to frighten them off your catch. You will soon know when you inspect the snare line if a fox has taken a rabbit from a wire, because all that will be left will be the rabbit's head.

You will also find at times that the whole wire has been snapped and the rabbit removed, which again is often the work of a fox; however, badgers do also have a tendency to help themselves to an easy meal, and will take a rabbit from a wire and will often pull the whole wire apart in the process.

My final comment concerning snaring is to say that if you *are* going to do it, make sure that you pick up *all* your wires on completion of your set. It is essential that you do not leave any behind, because if stock is then grazed on the area you have set and you have left a wire down, any livestock risks being caught. You must pick up your wires without fail!

Cage Traps for Rabbits

If you are dealing with areas where snaring is not practical, such as gardens or smallholdings where there may be a lot of stock or pets around, then a useful alternative may be to use a live-catch cage trap.

These are made for a variety of different quarry species ranging from rats to foxes, and are very easy to obtain from just about any agricultural supplier (I have even found them in garden centres!). The rabbit cage is a simple-to-operate trap whereby the rabbit enters the cage, and in doing so treads on a plate that slips the door and thus holds the rabbit within. In the summer time it is quite easy to catch rabbits in cage traps without bait, although most of these rabbits will be small ones.

To catch rabbits in the winter, or adult rabbits at any time of the year, you will need to bait your traps in order to have any chance of luring rabbits into them. You will also need to site your traps in suitable locations: there is no point in just putting them down anywhere. I would suggest setting them either around the rabbits' burrows, or around areas where you can see there is current rabbit damage; this could be along flower borders in gardens or on a lawn that is being dug up. You will need to bait your traps with a food source that is going to appeal to the rabbits more than the food they are already eating. I find the best bait is an equal mix of chopped fresh carrot and

A cage trap set besides a burrow.

cabbage mixed with some shelled peanuts or horse nuts, and if possible something that will really pull them in is a game feed or horse feed, ideally one with an aniseed smell to it.

Before baiting your traps, leave them in the area you wish to trap, but closed, so that the scent on them has a chance to dissipate; at the same time scatter some of your bait around the outside of the traps, and take heed as to whether it is taken over a couple of days. If it is, then add some more, and after another day or two put some into the trap in front and behind the kick plate. This done, you will hopefully find a rabbit or two caught the next day. If the bait is not taken, then move your traps a few yards and try them until it *is* taken.

I run half-a-dozen cage traps on a 7-acre patch that I keep my child's horse on, and normally by moving the traps fifty or so yards a week can continually catch a brace of bunnies a day. I must add, however, that this area is overrun with rabbits, and I have tried cages before on areas with fewer rabbits with much less effect.

As with snares, you must check your cages at least twice daily, and you must also ensure that any rabbits caught are humanely despatched as soon as you discover them.

Trapping in the Long Term

The two types of trapping already discussed are ideal for the hobbyist rabbit catcher who just runs a set of wires over the weekend or a few cages that he checks daily – but what if you decide to run some traps on a more permanent scale?

Trapping rabbits regularly can prove a good way to control them, but be warned: it takes up a lot of time, and is not something I would advise doing on a whim. As you will now be well aware, you will need to check your traps every day, and ideally twice daily, and if you are running a lot of traps over a large area, this will take up a great deal of time even if you are doing this by driving round in a car.

I used to trap a lot when I had the time to do it, and would run two types of trap: spring traps and drop traps. However, I was not just trapping for rabbits, but was also trying to pick up small vermin, so I used Fenn traps in marks 6 and 4. The Fenn trap is a spring-operated trap and works on the principle that the intended quarry stands on a kick plate in between the sprung jaws, and then triggers the jaws and becomes caught. These are the most commonly used traps. These days there are other traps including the body gripper and the rabbit Imbra trap, but I must confess that I have not used these widely, so will only describe using the Fenn trap.

Tunnel Traps

The mark 4 Fenn is not designed solely as a rabbit trap, but also for small vermin, taking a variety of quarry ranging from rats and squirrels to stoats and weasels. Of course during the summer months if you are catching rabbits for pest control it will be suitable to take small rabbits; but in my opinion the trap is not really big enough to take adult rabbits with the best results. This said, I have caught large rabbits in mark 4s, but have not set them intentionally to do this, and much prefer to use the mark 6 Fenn, a purpose-designed rabbit trap. The mark 4 is best used as a tunnel trap, and for best effect should be set in a man-made tunnel. The most common plan is to make a tunnel and to situate it in a location that vermin will pass through. This generally means making tunnels along hedge lines or fence lines, or on the corner of gateways, as all of these places are favourite crossing points for vermin.

Most small vermin, including rabbits, will always run along a fence or hedge line, given the opportunity, and a well positioned tunnel is very inviting. The tunnel must look inviting or it will not be of any use. Make sure you make the entrance and entry to the tunnel look natural and used, and don't simply assume that you can stick a rough tunnel up, pop a trap in it, and expect to catch. If you are setting a tunnel trap along a stone wall, make the tunnel blend in. Try to make it with a stone shell so that it looks like part of the wall and not foreign to its environment; the same applies if you are setting it by a log pile or on a hedge line: make sure the tunnel fits the surroundings.

I always made my tunnels out of cheap timber so that I had a solid shell; I could then attach my trap to the timber with a good chain so that it could not be removed. The tunnel could then be positioned and I could cover the timber with whatever material I wanted, so that it blended in. In this manner, when I was trapping regularly, I would set up about two hundred tunnels over an 800-acre estate. I would run a hundred traps and would alternate them through the tunnels on a fortnightly basis so that each area was continuously trapped, and no area was left untended for too long a time. In this manner, and checking my

An overview of a set Fenn trap.

traps at dawn and dusk, I regularly accounted for stoats, rats and squirrels.

As my traps were always out they were constantly exposed to the elements, and so any tell-tale scent was quickly obscured; furthermore, I always ensured that when set in a tunnel they were slightly dug in and had a light sprinkle of soil on top of them so they were not visible to even the most wary of weasels! A final tip with using tunnel traps is that to stop predators and larger quarry species from trying to poke into your tunnel and remove your catch, it can be worthwhile to cut a few lengths of elder or hazel: they do not need to be more than a centimetre thick and a few centimetres long, but can be used at the front of your tunnels to partially block the entrance. Small vermin will be able to push through, but larger vermin will not.

Tunnel traps are therefore suitable for picking up the occasional bunny, especially when a lot of three-quarter-grown ones are about; but in general, the best trap for serious rabbiting has to be the Fenn mark 6. This is generally best used in the mouth of a rabbit hole, and unlike the mark 4, in a natural hole and not in a man-made tunnel. However, this type of trapping is really very time-consuming, and best left to the professional rabbit catcher.

To trap inside the rabbit holes means that you will need to ensure that the trap is fitted inside the hole and is not left in the open where it could catch any sort of wandering animal: this is totally illegal – as is setting traps on poles to catch birds or vermin.

Another tip is that there is no point setting one trap in a burrow of fifty holes: to work properly you really need to trap every hole in your chosen warren. Again,

this takes a lot of time, but can produce some excellent returns. My advice to you if you are trapping on an *ad hoc* basis is to stick to tunnel trapping around burrows, but to use mark 6 Fenns as opposed to mark 4s if your intended quarry is to be rabbit.

I have very successfully set up artificial tunnels around rabbit burrows that I knew held huge numbers of rabbits, and over the course of two to three weeks have caught a rabbit in each trap, sometimes twice daily. If you watch rabbits cavorting on burrows, especially large ones – and by 'large' I am talking about two hundred holes plus – you will often see them dive in and out of holes in play, and if your tunnels are well set up, rabbits will keep popping in and out of them, and will keep getting caught. I have had very good results in this manner, with only six or a dozen traps set up, and have managed to reduce otherwise difficult populations. You can, of course, set your traps in standard tunnels, but remember that the mark 6 is slightly higher and wider than the mark 4, and that your tunnels will need to be larger to accommodate the trap.

The Box or Drop Trap

The final trap to mention is, in my opinion, the best of the best when it comes to rabbit trapping, and is another live-catch trap. The box or drop trap is extremely simple to make, though it can be bought, if you so wish. It is also simplicity itself to set up, consisting of a box that is set into the ground with the top of it level to the ground. On top of the box is a pivoted board. The rabbit runs on to the board, which tilts downwards, depositing the said rabbit into the box that is situated underneath it. The rabbit is then secure until you remove it from the box. Because this trap is a live cage trap it also has the advantage that you can remove and release any rabbits that you do not wish to cull, for instance milky does or youngsters that you wish to release until they are of a more usable size.

As with tunnel traps, the best location for drop traps is along natural runs such as hedge and fence lines; it is also advisable to make a tunnel on top of the drop board to really make the trap effective.

Rabbits will naturally head for the tunnel when threatened or when on the move, and box traps with a tunnel on top seem to work very much better than those without.

Again, when I used to trap I often set up fifty or so box traps on an estate I covered, and they never let me down. Of course it took a lot of work to set them up as they had to be dug in and, as with all the trapping, checking them took a lot of time; but the results were well worth it in the long run.

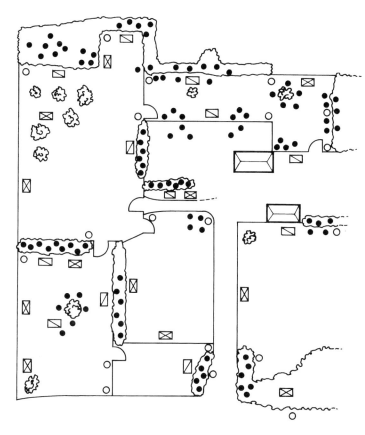

A trapping plan consisting of a mix of tunnel traps, cage traps and box traps.

◰ cage traps being rotated
⊠ box traps
O tunnel traps

CHAPTER 12

RUNNING DOGS AND RABBITS

The second subject that I feel is worth a few pages is something as close to my heart and as important to me as my netting, and that is the use of lurchers for taking rabbits. I have left this until last because I feel it is important to show that this is a separate matter to the subject of dogs for long netting. As already mentioned, I am not a good dog trainer, and do not feel I have the knowledge to write at length about how to train them, or make them perform well in the field; there are plenty of others who have this knowledge. However, if you enjoy netting and rabbiting, a basic insight into the world of the lurcher as a rabbiting dog may well give you another line of sport that you might wish to pursue.

As I have mentioned, my current dog is a lurcher, and at the moment I am enjoying some of the best rabbiting I have ever had with him. Certainly there are other dogs that can be used for rabbiting, and I am not trying to undervalue them by not mentioning them; but I find that as an all-round ferreting and lamping dog, the lurcher is ideal. They are not easy to train, and I can certainly vouch that a sight hound to sight hound cross such as mine (a 'long dog' to the purist) is a lot harder to educate than a collie cross sight hound or similar. This

is probably why so many lurchers are found in rescue centres, and are regularly passed on from one owner to another; however, if you can put up with the difficult times – and speaking from experience, the first three years with a lurcher really *are* difficult – the rewards afterwards are well worth it.

It takes time and patience to teach a lurcher the vagaries of this sport, and you will have to accept that if a dog is to make any progress, you will have to let it go on some rabbits – and you will lose some. Some people teach their lurcher to hold rabbits in a purse or long net until they can get to it; others teach it to watch the burrow whilst they remove the rabbit from the nets – but the key is, to teach the dog to do what *you* want, and to stick to your own preference.

I have taught my lurcher to hold rabbits in the net whilst I get to them, and also to run on any rabbits that slip the nets – and as far as I am concerned, this is when the real joy of lurcher work comes into play. Watching a dog of such stature – no matter what sort it is – twist and turn on a bolted rabbit, and then grab it just before it dives for cover, is something I never get bored watching. And of course lurchers are not only of use when ferreting, but can perform various other tasks.

The author's lurcher out for a day's ferreting.

Returning to hand with the catch.

I enjoy nothing more in the summer than setting forth with my dog at first light and letting him run through thick cover and flush out hedges. This really seems to test his ability, and he does earn every rabbit. To be honest I never thought he would work as well as he does now, because in the past he only had to *see* a rabbit sitting out in the open and would charge full pelt at it, without any thought of what to do then; and it took quite a few trips out before he came anywhere near catching a rabbit in the daytime by bushing and flushing. At present

during our walk-out trips we normally get a brace of rabbits at least, and I still get a thrill when he suddenly stops, pointing towards a clump of brambles, and then suddenly strikes and emerges with a rabbit in his grasp.

What type the lurcher is will to a certain extent dictate what it can do; for instance, a smooth-haired dog with a thin coat is not going to work as well in thick cover as one with a heavier, rougher coat. The current trend in rabbiting lurchers seems to be for the Bedlington x Whippet, which produces a small but plucky dog

The dog connecting with a rabbit that has just been flushed from a seat in the field.

that is not scared to get stuck in. It is not, however, my favourite cross, and I still prefer the Collie × Greyhound: to my mind this cross has just that little more brain, and is well suited to most sorts of rabbiting. As already mentioned, my own lurcher is a Deerhound × Greyhound of giant proportions, more suited to coursing than to ferreting and bushing – but as I am discovering, he is more than up to the task of rabbiting, despite his size.

I believe that as long as you train your lurcher to obey the basics, such as retrieving, sitting and staying, and of course coming to hand, you are well on the way to having a dog that, no matter what sort of cross you have, will do what you want it to, and catch your chosen quarry. You must also be sure to stock-train your dog, as a dog – and especially a lurcher – that takes to chasing stock is no good to anyone, and will land you in nothing but trouble.

To my mind it is also crucial that your lurcher is taught to jump well. I never understood this until I started to train my own dog and began to appreciate just how fast he moves, and realized that if he

The author's lurcher out working; the field holds several hundred sheep, thus indicating the importance of a dog being stock trained.

could not jump, and jump well, it would be only a matter of time before he collided with something and killed himself. My lurcher also accompanies me on shooting trips; he will mark and retrieve wounded game, and is now proving a worthy companion, always by my side when out in the field. Marking seems to be something that a good dog will teach itself to do in time, and again is very useful – in fact, I would say crucial – in a dog that is being used for ferreting.

A dog that marks will indicate to you if a rabbit is in a burrow by giving you some sort of signal: some will tilt their head slightly, whilst others lift a paw – but avoid a dog that tries to stick its head down a hole, as this ruins the burrow and only persuades the inhabitants to sit tight. As I have said, I don't know how a dog learns to mark properly; I may be lucky, but all my dogs have learnt to mark in the course of a season or two's ferreting, and have never lied at the task. I know that if my dog says a burrow is inhabited, then there will be at least one rabbit in it, and on every occasion that I have gone against him, I have soon been proved to be in the wrong, as the burrow has sure enough been empty.

I believe that the key to working well with a dog only comes when you can trust your dog and your dog trusts you, and this is something that I feel is especially prominent in lurchers. I find that I have an almost telepathic link with my dogs, and that I and my dogs know when the time is right for them to work freely, to their true ability. This is especially noticeable in the lamping field. Lurchers are renowned for their speed and agility, and lamping has to be the one task that any lurcher can grow into with a little practice; in fact, I would go as far as to say that even the worst lurcher could pick up lamped rabbits after a few trips out.

Lamping

The idea of lamping is simple. A powerful lamp is used at night to pick out rabbits grazing, and the dog is then allowed to run on the rabbit. When a lurcher is first used it will, as with ferreting, lose a good few rabbits; but with practice it will soon learn how to overcome rabbits that are in the beam of the lamp. Instead of running straight at a lamped rabbit, a good dog will run alongside the beam, then cut in on the rabbit and snatch it up. This is an amazing sight to see, and I never tire of it; I don't go lamping that often – perhaps once a week – but I enjoy every second of it.

As with netting, the best nights are those with a slight wind to carry your scent, and a little light rain or drizzle is also ideal. As already mentioned, my own charge has now finally, after two-and-a-half seasons, really taken to lamping, and goes out without being on a lead, and can be trusted to walk alongside me and to

run on rabbits that are lamped up. To me this is really remarkable, in that eight months ago he was so poor at lamping that I never thought he would master it even on a slip-lead, let alone off the lead altogether; perhaps he is finally maturing into the skills that in retrospect I pushed on him too early in his life. I mentioned earlier that my lurcher was nineteen months old and rather slow to develop – well, he is now two and a half, and is proving his worth above all of my expectations. I have not yet used him in any serious manner with long nets, but I believe from the way he is going that he will be a useful netting dog when I give him the opportunity to work with nets in the next few months.

In summary, I believe that a lurcher is the ideal rabbiting companion, and in my experience will be loyal to you in a way that can seldom be found in other breeds (I have had a variety of other dogs including spaniels and other gundogs). It is just sad that as a breed the lurcher is so misunderstood and mistreated by so many. They do take a long time to mature, and are demanding to train, so that although many people are attracted to them, they give up on the dog before it has a chance to display its true potential.

A small number of people still run lurchers, but they don't train them in basic obedience, nor do they care for them correctly. They expect their dogs to run without exception, and never give a thought to their health care or needs. These people are best avoided, although they are easily found; they are like the pub netter who is happy to tell the story of a hundred rabbits caught two nights previously, but strangely never has the occasional brace going spare. (You will, of course, know that two nights previously was a still night with a full moon, and the only thing worth catching was the end of the film you wanted to watch.)

Take my advice, keep your rabbiting and netting quiet from these sorts, and keep your lurchers away from these people, as they have an uncanny way of interfering with your activities and telling you how to do everything when, if the truth be told, they do not know what they are doing themselves. Finally, as with ferrets, remember that a dog will be with you for a long time, and there is more to it than just the rabbiting. You will need to house it and feed it, and pay for any vets' bills – which could be costly if your lurcher is injured out lamping or generally in the field. I would strongly suggest doing your homework as to what type will be best for you, and whether you truly have the time to put into a dog before buying one.

What to Do with Your Catch

I feel it is a fitting tribute to our quarry to mention briefly just what you can do with your quarry once you have caught it. First, you must ensure that any rabbits you catch are paunched as soon as is feasibly possible after they have been caught. If you leave the guts in the carcase too long, especially in the summer months, they will taint the meat and make the flesh unusable.

You must ensure that your paunch is suitably disposed of, and is not left scattered across the field you have caught the rabbits in. I would suggest that you find or dig a hole and bury the paunch. The liver and kidney can be kept for animal food for your dogs or ferrets, as can the heart and lungs. For the novice, the easiest way to paunch a rabbit is to hold it by the back legs and to slit the underside from the groin area towards the centre of the rib cage. If this is done with a good sharp knife you will then be able to place your fingers behind the stomach and slip the paunch out with a quick flick of the wrist.

Once the rabbits have been paunched, they can be stored for a few hours by hanging them by the back legs in a cool place away from flies that could again in the summer taint the meat and make it useless. If your rabbits are for your own use they can then be skinned off and either portioned, or left as a whole carcase for consumption for yourselves or your animals. Alternatively you could sell your catch to a licensed game dealer or butcher; prices tend to vary, but at the time of writing I can get £1.20 for a freshly netted rabbit in the skin. I have a very good system worked out with two local butchers, who take my rabbits from me and then exchange them for meat at the above value per rabbit; by doing this the family never goes hungry, and there is always a good mix of meat in my freezer.

If you intend to eat your catch yourself, there are a variety of rabbit recipes at your fingertips. I have enjoyed curried rabbit, rabbit pie, battered rabbit and – one of my favourites – roast rabbit stuffed with sausage meat and vegetables. The choice of recipes is up to you, but rabbit is very versatile and is quite a lean meat, so in my opinion is a healthy choice for all the family.

My final word on this subject is to make sure that you are aware of the various rules and regulations relating to the storage and selling of game so that you do not get caught out and accidentally break the law.

Bon appétit – and happy hunting and eating!

GLOSSARY

Anchor pin Metal peg used to anchor each end of a long net in place.

Bag/bagging Term used to describe excess netting in a net, also known as 'slack'.

Ball up/balling up Term used to describe a rabbit caught in a net.

BASC The British Association of Shooting and Conservation.

Bolt shot/bolt shooting Alternative method to using nets when ferreting incorporating the use of a shotgun to shoot the 'bolted rabbits' that the ferrets flush from underground.

Box trap Live catch trap that consists of a boxed compartment and a trap-door catch method.

Bunny The term given to a young rabbit.

Burrow Underground tunnel network inhabited by rabbits, normally consisting of from two to thirty holes.

CA The Countryside Alliance.

Cage trap Live catch trap consisting of a cage holding area and a spring-loaded entry.

Chinning Term used to describe despatching a rabbit.

Clove hitch Knot used to attach a net to the end ring holding it in place.

Coney Another term for a rabbit or rabbits.

Cotton A natural twine that can be used to construct nets (depending on thickness).

Draw cord The cord running around a net to support it or attach it in place, also known as a running cord or 'runner'.

Drop net Long net supported on a pole and slider system that allows the net to be dropped between the rabbits and their burrows/home ground.

Fenn trap Spring-operated trap set in a tunnel to catch small vermin.

Gate net Net used to block a gateway, generally to catch rabbits and hares.

Ground Game Act Act originally introduced in 1880 to allow tenant farmers more freedom to legally control rabbits damaging their crops.

Hazel The wood taken from the hazel tree used to construct net pegs and snare pegs. Best cut in the winter and allowed to dry and season until spring.

Hedge net Net similar to a purse net and used to block gaps in a hedgerow.
NB In some areas of the country this could be known as a stop net or ditch net.

Hemp A natural twine used to make nets.

Hob Term used to describe a male ferret.

Jute A twine similar in colour and texture to hemp but of a greater reduced quality.

Long net Net measuring between 25 and 200yd long used to catch rabbits.

Lurcher Cross-bred dog usually consisting of either Greyhound/Whippet or Collie base lines, and often used to hunt rabbits.

Mesh-board Small piece of board used as a spacing device when making nets. The size of the mesh will indicate the size of the mesh on the net.

Myxomatosis Disease that affects rabbits and no other species; also known as 'myxi'.

Nylon Twine that is man-made and used in the construction of nets. Comes in a variety of mediums and is also used as draw cord on nets.

Paunching Term used to describe gutting a rabbit.

Peg Used to support a net or to hold a net in place; generally wooden, but can b found in a variety of mediums. Vary i size depending on the intended use.

Permanent set net A long net that has it support pegs attached to it permanently

Pre-set net A long net that has the net ting tied to its draw cord at intervals fo ease.

Priest Small club-like instrument usual ly in wood or antler, with a weighted lea end; used to despatch small game/vermin

Purse net Net used to block a rabbi hole, normally when ferreting. Consists o a net set on a drawer cord with two en rings and a peg holding the drawer cord

Run Name given to the tramway creat ed by rabbits regularly running along th same line.

Runner *see* draw cord.

Running cord Long cord held betwee two people and used to drag across a fiel to flush rabbits back towards the lon nets; also known as a drag, or bant cord.

Set The term used to describe the placin of a long net between the quarry and it home.

Slack netting *see* bag/bagging.

Slider The part of a drop net used to slid down the support pole and to hold th net.

Snare A wire noose-style trap used to 'snare' rabbits, generally made from brass wire.

Spool A ball of twine of any type wound on to a reel.

Spun nylon A woollen form of nylon used to construct nets.

Tealer A support stake usually made of thin wire or elder/hazel, which is used to support a snare's noose.

Twine The name used to generally describe the material used to knit a net with; this could be nylon/cotton/hemp or any other twine.

VHD Viral haemorrhagic disease.

Warren The name given to a rabbit burrow that numbers generally over twenty holes.

Warrener The name used in the past to describe a full-time rabbit catcher.

Wire Another term for a snare.

INDEX